WOW!

Women of Destiny

WOW! Women of Destiny

How To Create A Life Full of
Passion, Purpose and Power In God

Earma Brown
Pink Tree Publishing
Dallas, Texas

All Scripture quotations are from the King James Version of the New Scofield Bible. 1967 Printed by Oxford University Press. All New Testament definitions are taken from W.E. Vines Dictionary of New Testament Words.

ISBN-10: 09895524-6-2
ISBN-13: 978-0-9895524-6-2

Published in the United States of America.

Early Praise for the WOW! Women Trilogy of Books

Earma, I wanted you to know how much I have been enjoying reading your WOW! Women book. It literally has been like God told you to write it just for me. I can now identify how much I have dealt with rejection in my life. Just the other day, I found myself recognizing the spirit of rejection. I immediately thought of you and your book. I responded with a right response: I repented and forgave the person. Thank you for writing this book... —*Charlette Lakey*

Absolutely!! I would love to bless my entire book club with a copy and we will make it the highlight for our first meeting. We would certainly love for you to join us for the discussion as it really feed my spirit when I read it for the first time. It is truly needed within our club ministry right now so it will be my absolute pleasure... to purchase books...as I will gift the books to them as a stocking stuffer for Christmas. —*Jackie, Girlfriends, Book Club President*

It's a must read because, she taps into your mind: meaning she talks about things that you have questioned yourself about, makes you think about things that you have said or thought and you know that you shouldn't have said or though lol... she helps us to tap into and appreciate who God has made us to be, the book is very enlightening. Thank you Earma :))) —*Kitty*

Thank you for the book. It has given me so much hope. As I sat and read WOW! my mind went back to my life when I first got married and I began to read my Bible and God gave me a new life and now my life could not be better. I wake up in the morning and say Thank you Jesus! —*Love, your Aunt Samella*

I loved the book. I ordered some to give to young ladies so they would be encouraged. I am going to spread the good news to women at my church also…because this book is definitely Good news. —unknown

Earma, you outdid yourself. WOW! is a must read for ALL women. I read it and it was a fantastic book. I can't wait for the next one. You keep empowering women. I can't say enough good things about WOW! I truly loved it. —*Vickye Allison Frazier*

Just stopping by to congratulate you on WOW! books. Excellent book so far. I've been reading Women of Worth since I left Chicago. I plan to finish it tonight (especially luv the chapter on "Unlocking Your Potential." I've already promised to give it to Kesha once I finish it as well as recommend it to other females within my social network. Personally, I think this book should be on Oprah's book of the month. Keep making the family proud with your superb writing and inspirational messages!!!! —*Jacque Morrison*

Thank you for teaching the class "WOW! Women Encouraging Women to Their Purpose and Destiny" We have been hearing good reports of the blessing you were to your students. We appreciate your faithfulness and service to the Lord in teaching His children. We know many have been blessed by your obedience to serve Him. —*Late Melinda Manning, Pastor, Covenant Church, Carrollton, Texas*

Earma, I cannot express enough to you the timeliness of this message! Many, many women will be blessed and grow through this teaching. You are out at the threshold of a great and mighty "new thing" that God is doing for His women who search after His heart!! You are blessed – you are anointed. You are on your way. I considered it a great pleasure that you allowed me the privilege to review your material. —*Darla Knoll, Former Women's Ministry Coordinator, Covenant Church, Carrollton, Texas.*

Dearest Earma, thank you so much for sharing your life, your heart and your wisdom. But especially, thank you for your love! Thank you for building us up. —*Mary, WOW Class attendee.*

I look forward to WOW, Women of Destiny the class. It has been a blessing in my life. Thank you. —*Illya Roberts*

Earma, it has been a blessing to have you as a teacher these last few weeks. We appreciated your sweet spirit! Since you are such a giver we felt led to give you a token of our love for you... —*Jane & Cleo, WOW class attendees.*

I've struggled with so many of the same issues that I was encouraged to see someone bold enough to write about it. I enjoyed the class and I'm looking forward to the books. —*Bettie Cormel, WOW class attendee.*

To add your testimony or positive comment to this list for next book, please visit Earma at http://wowontheweb.com/testimonies/

Dedication

I dedicate this book to my beloved sisters and brothers:

Oneadia Kates, Marie Toms, Cecelia Tasby, Marilyn Worsham, Linda Howard, Minnie Broadway, Charlette Lakey, Kitty Brown and dear brothers Lenner Broadway, Bernard Broadway, Robert Broadway.

Thank you for your support and encouragement through the years. When I succeeded you cheered and when I missed the mark you rallied in kindness, when I fell short you extended a helping hand and when I am victorious, you can be sure you will be invited to celebrate at the party and share in the bounty.

Set up road signs; put up guideposts. Take note of the highway, the road that you take. —*Jeremiah 31:21*

Acknowledgements

Special thanks to all the women and men that have imparted to my life and to this message. You have helped divide my sorrows, multiply my joys and participated in my victories:

My husband and sons: Varn Brown Sr., Khrystopher Brown and Varn Brown, Jr.

My Mothers: Parlee Broadway, Betty Brown (Ma-Betty), Vivian Brown (Aunt Suge), Pastor Kathy Hayes (Mom Katie), Pastor Jessye Ruffin (Mom-Ruffin), Pastor Kittie Cochran (Mama Kittie), Mrs. Inga Davis (Mama Inga) and the late Mrs. Palmer Chandler (Mother Chandler).

Women of Destiny Who Inspire Me: Melissa Kates Brown, Nanette Walker, Amanda Bell, Shaunta Agueman, Jacqueline Morrison, Cheryl Finney, Lelah, Christina Broadway and Jo Brown. I am grateful to each of you for your support and encouragement in the task God has given me.

Thank you for believing in me.

Book two:

WOW! Women of Destiny

How To Create A Life Full Of Passion, Purpose And Power In God

Preface   xix

Chapter One: Going To Your Destiny   23
A Woman's Predestination

How did a girl at seventeen lead an army of hardheaded Frenchmen to victory in two short years? Joan of Arc gained a sense of destiny by realizing the brevity of life. A voice told her that France would change forever in two short years then a country, a nation, a people would be lost UNLESS she acted now. She did what we must all do. She learned the power of now.

Chapter Two: Walking Through Your Process With Patience   39
A Woman's Pursuit of God's Presence

What did Rahab, a former Jerichoian prostitute do that got her an honorable mention in the genealogy of Christ, landed her in the Christian faith hall of fame and changed her future forever? The king and the whole city trembled in fear at news of the plans of the Israelis and their God. But Rahab alone confessed and believed, "Your God is God!" She stepped out and pursued God in a way that saved her entire family and sealed her destiny.

Chapter Three: Seizing The Season   57
A Woman's Propitious Power of Preparation

An eclectic group of twelve people were looking for their Kairos moment. What virtue did they all commonly need to obtain it? Five out of the ten women used its power; so did Michael Jordan and Thomas Edison. What kept Jordan going through the failed baskets he made to perfect his game?

How did Edison continue in the face of countless botched experiments to gain a successful invention? And why did only five women enter in when the other five were left out with nothing to show for their effort? Seven of twelve used the precocious power of preparation.

Chapter Four: Turning Your Troubles Into Triumph   73
A Woman's Fiery Passion Points To Purpose

Candy Lightner was considered a normal housewife with children. So, what caused her to almost single-handedly change a nation's complacent thinking about drinking while driving? Her twelve-year old daughter, Cari was killed by a drunk driver. Armed with a fiery passion to help other mothers face similar tragedies, she formed MADD (Mothers Against Drunk Driving) and in the process turned her troubles into triumph.

Chapter Five: Receiving Your Appointment From God   87
A Woman's Wild And Precocious Purpose Leads To Power

She was born when it was not considered proper for a young woman to become a nurse. Her parents forbade it, thinking her a wild swan among ducks, society frowned upon it, and the medical professionals ignored it. Yet, Florence Nightingale changed the way the world viewed nursing and women. Where did she begin? She received her appointment from God.

Chapter Six: Praying Through To Power   107
A Woman's Prevailing Prayer Power

The call of God and her destiny was wrapped into the development of this virtue. After years of trial sent to help her develop it, Kathryn Kulhman is considered the beloved woman of God extraordinaire because of her faith, perseverance and relationship with the Holy Spirit. How did she develop such prayer power with God and encouraged others to come on the journey? She persevered and found power with God.

Chapter Seven: Fulfilling Your Passion, Purpose...   125
A Woman's Power Propels Her Destiny

They were pastors with a gift of love destined to be God's ministers of reconciliation. Tragically, the husband began to drink. After years of violence and bitterness, merely traces of their destiny remained. They might have fulfilled their destiny, if they had only known about the destiny thieves sent to pull the plug on their purpose and steal their happy ending.

Chapter Eight: Leaving A Legacy... 143

A Woman's Pattern of Power Perpetuates Her Legacy

A little girl was born in a time of turmoil for Israel. She was an orphan with no future and no destiny. Yet, through the hand of God she was raised to fame, power and destiny. Or so it seemed, what happened next could have turned her bright future to darkness. She and her nation fasted, prayed and acted in the power of God. In the process, she learned a secret that brought salvation to her nation with an unexpected upset of her enemies' plans so powerful that her pattern echoes through the centuries for generations to come. She learned the power of God's recompense.

Summary   159

Bibliography   165

Discussion Guide   167

About Author   173

Other WOW! Books & Resources   175

.

Preface

Dear Woman of Destiny:

Welcome to the second study in the WOW! Women Series. All three books were written as stand-alone studies. I offer a little of my history and testimony for those of you joining us for the first time. When I began writing the WOW! Women material, I was reaching for women delivered from abusive lifestyles who wanted to rebuild their self-image and life in God.

Yet, Father God burned into my mind one evening before a Bible study I was teaching for a rowdy group of maximum security inmates at the Dallas County Jail, "Tell them they are WOW! Women of Worth." I went on to develop a WOW! Women of Worth class.

After teaching the WOW! Women classes in the Dallas County Jails and my local church, I discovered another facet of what God wanted to do with this message. Yes, women were gaining a right image (a biblical perspective) of themselves. But the class sessions, books and now the events have become a time of women from any background with different struggles coming together as women encouraging one another to victory and destiny in their lives.

Over twenty years ago, I was a victim of spouse abuse. On the outside except for being abnormally thin, I looked normal. Yet, on the inside, I was wounded and walking around humped over with my arms hanging to the ground. I used to drive by the city's heavily shaded cemetery not far from my workplace and envy the people lying out there under the trees in peace.

I thought often about giving up thinking, "It must be nice to be in total rest without pretense and no wounds to hide." Yet, something within me would whisper, "Your life is not always going to be like this." I now know that something was someone, the Holy Spirit, keeping a spark of hope alive in me.

My God has been faithful for my life is nothing like it used to be. During that season of my life, I moved as far away as I could get (about 600 miles) from my then hopeless life. The rest is history and a long story; after years of denying me a divorce, the abusive husband, eventually divorced me. I recommitted my life to Jesus, later that same year.

My Lord and I began putting the fragmented pieces of my life together. He began walking me through steps to healing and wholeness. He has since rewarded my faith with a loving husband and filled my heart with compassion for His wonderful creation WOMAN.

From this compassion, the message of 'WOW! Women' was birthed. The material was developed from the healing and process it has taken for me to think right about myself, and not only connect, but walk in my own destiny. God began to develop his truth in me that became strategies to becoming the women of victory and destiny He designed for us all to become.

My goal is to bring a message of hope and vision to those who hunger for God's destiny and purpose in their life. In part one of this series of books, we uncovered a trail of seven biblical truths that show value in a woman's life by helping us answer the four classic questions of life afresh and sometimes for the first time: 'Where did I come from?' Who am I?' "Why am I here?' and just as importantly 'Where am I going?' It was quite a journey.

Now, in WOW! Women of Destiny, we continue this biblical trail leading to our passion, purpose and the power to fulfill our destiny. So, each chapter has been designed to leave every woman with a sense of destiny which will help her discover and fulfill her God given purpose.

If you journeyed with me through the Women of Worth book, you know that I usually give the blueprint for the next teaching in the last chapter. So, the last chapter of this book is Leaving a Legacy then enters WOW! Women of Legacy. If not already, you can send for a copy of that book on wowontheweb.com, Amazon.com or get it free when you sign up for a WOW! Women Global membership. http://wowwomenglobal.com

Back to this book, in *WOW! Women of Destiny* I use destiny terminology. The individual lessons are introduced or reinforced to build the faith of God's woman in realizing her value and fulfilling her destiny. In each A Sign Post Of Destiny and A Step Towards Destiny section throughout the book, I aspire to draw a map respectively using a woman's predestination, pursuit, preparation, passion, purpose, prevailing prayer and power as instructional signposts along the road to destiny.

None of us want to stumble and miss our destiny. We want to run our God-appointed course and finish it in victory. Therefore, the Strengthening Your Step portion was written to concisely emphasize points to strengthen our walk toward destiny.

Realizing the world is not a perfect place but one of struggle and conflict of opposing forces, I have chosen to present contrasting aspects of the seven steps of destiny in each Crossroads to Destiny segment. I seek to see women know there will be challenges in their lives yet at the same time remain confident that with God on their side they are well able to overcome every challenging circumstance. Can't you hear the voice of wisdom and understanding? She is standing at the city gates and at every crossroad, and at the door of every house. Listen to what she says.

Recognizing faith without works is dead, the Destiny Summary and Challenge Exercises sections are designed to sum it all up and help you apply God's Word in your life.

Finally, you might know it's now a tradition, my faith always makes an appointment with Father God for our time together. I believe; He will again meet us in each chapter and by His Spirit shatter images that say no to your prosperity, purpose, power and pattern in God.

He has already said YES and AMEN to every promise. So, come on; let's walk together through WOW! Women of Destiny to fulfill every plan, purpose and destiny He has reserved for our lives. (Jeremiah 29:11)

Earma Brown

Chapter One

Going to Your Destiny

A Woman's Predestination

But the good woman—what a different story! For the good woman—the blameless, the upright, the woman of peace—she has a wonderful future ahead for her. For her there is a happy ending. –Psalms 37:37 TLB

*J*oan of Arc claimed to be a messenger from God sent to restore the royal family's rule and kingdom. With a clear purpose and sense of destiny, she did just that in two short years. The movie, The Messenger released in the year 2000 brought renewed attention to the story of Joan of Arc.

French saint and national heroine, called the Maid of Orleans, Jeanne D'Arc was the daughter of a farmer of Domremy on the border of Champagne and Lorraine.

The story says that Joan began hearing voices, at a very young age. At first, they only told her non-threatening things like, "Be a good girl and obey your parents."

Then as she got older their intensity and sense of urgency increased until eventually they told her the time was now to act for in a few short years everything would be changed in the nation.

Theologians and historians alike still argue whether the voice was from God but one thing we can gain from the life of Joan is that she had a strong sense of destiny and purpose in her life.

We can know that France was a changed nation because of her. That same sense of destiny and purpose is applicable to us in our world today.

What is our destiny or final outcome? God has already decided that our final outcome is to be made into the image of His Son, Jesus. (Romans 8:29) It has been pre-destined (lovingly arranged beforehand) that we would be adopted as children of God through His Son Jesus. Recognize your destiny as a believer. When we receive Christ, we have connected with the first part of our destiny (desired and expected end).

The second part is the getting in agreement with the purpose and plan of God. Our agreement becomes our choice and our obedience to God's will. The Apostle Paul phrased it like this, "For we are God's workmanship, created in Christ Jesus to do good works, which God prepared in advance for us to do. (Eph. 2:10).

Have you wondered why the Cinderella story and others like it has such a timeless appeal to many? It's because Father God has put in each of us a desire, a dream, a hope for a bright future and a happy ending. It touches the deep-seated hunger to be and do what we have been destined for.

God has made arrangements to satisfy that hunger in us. He has planned our bright future and happy ending, essentially our destiny. The prophet Jeremiah proclaiming God's heart said, "I know the plans I have for you; plans of good and not evil, to give you a hope and future."

To expand our understanding of God's thoughts toward us, let's examine some terms used in the Scripture above. The word plan is defined as thoughts, blueprint, direction or purpose.

Hope is your expectancy of good, your dream, an expected end and even your purpose or destination. In addition, future is explained as your chance to succeed, your due season, your final outcome, your fate or simply destiny. (Webster's New World Dictionary and Thesaurus)

Let's take another look at what God said through the prophet Jeremiah using some of the definitive words above, "For I know the (blueprint, direction or purpose) that I have for you, saith the Lord, a (purpose) of peace and not evil, to give you (your expectancy of good, your dream, an expected end) and (your chance to succeed, your due season or destiny.)"

You see God has planted our dreams of good fortune and having a happy ending within us in seed form. Within each seed is the blueprint of our individual destiny, an expected end and even our bright future.

Join me as we uncover the biblical principles of developing the seeds of destiny given to each of us.

Sign Post to Destiny

Seven Assassins Sent To Kill Your Dream

The thief comes only to steal and kill and destroy; I have come that they may have life, and have it to the full. –John 10:10

Joan of Arc overcame tremendous obstacles and challenges to see the fulfillment of her dream, restoring the royal family to rule in France. Her dreams led her to oppose political and religious forces struggling to rule.

Her leadership and inspiration of her countrymen worked a miracle in France's history but led to her betrayal and execution by religious forces that used her claim of hearing voices as a point of condemnation. After she would not denounce the voices as evil, she was burned at the stake as a witch.

Wait! Before you get nervous about dying for your dream, perhaps you are like most of us. Your dream may not be leading you to die for a dream you believe but to live for the Christ you believe.

Has your dream been challenged with obstacles? Damaging circumstances, lack of funds, lack of support and interest, your status in life, your race or all of the above may act as winds of a storm against your dream.

The Apostle Paul said to the Corinthian Church, "Who cut in on you when you were doing so well?" Now I ask you, "What assassin has killed or attempted to cut off your dream."

We have been taught from the Word of God that Jesus came that we might have life and that more abundantly. The devil came to steal, kill and destroy. He will seek to take plunder and devour our future, our dream, our expected end and even our destiny.

In my own life, the weekend after I repented for burying my talent and decided to begin using my writing gifts and talents afresh, I made a commitment aloud before several people to begin writing whatever God put in my heart to write. In those days, I did most of my writing in long-hand for I did not own a personal computer.

My first project, I felt led to do was to volunteer the production of a newsletter for our jail ministry team. The next weekend, I fell asleep laying on my left hand and arm. I woke up in the middle of the night and began popping my hand and wrist trying to get feeling to return.

From that day forward, through almost nine months of excruciating pain every time I would move my writing hand I could feel something pop within my wrist. I went to doctor after doctor being diagnosed and prescribed medication to treat everything from carpal tunnel (tennis wrist) to arthritis with nothing helping.

Finally, after one day seeking God about receiving my healing I was in a medical clinic that happened to have a specialist in that day. I thought why not; I have seen everybody else. She seemed to know immediately what it was. She asked had I popped my wrist real hard playing sports.

I, instantly, remembered waking up that night I described earlier and popping my hand. I discovered half asleep, I had popped the tiny ligament that should ordinarily go between the small bones in my wrist out. It became inflamed and would not go back in.

So, each wrong movement caused the ligament to slide over the bone causing great pain. She wrapped my wrist, prescribed an anti-inflammatory and instructed me to rest my hand for two weeks.

A week or so later, my wrist was normal. Praise God! I can hear some of you saying so what did that have to with anything? Well, that circumstance created a challenge for my writing dream.

It posed the question would I keep my commitment to God about using my talents even when it was difficult. Or would I just put it back on the shelf. I chose to trust God and continue through the difficulty. I learned to write with my right hand and bought a computer while it worked out.

The problem was eventually revealed and fixed. I kept going through taking writing classes, to eventually teaching writing classes, writing books to publishing books…

Again, I ask what assassin has attempted to cut off your dream? We have been taught from the Word of God that Jesus came that we might have life more abundantly.

The devil came to steal, kill and destroy. He will seek to take plunder and devour our future and dream many times before it's birthed. So, let's take a moment and examine some things that might seek to assassinate your dream.

1.   **Fear.** Are you afraid to fail? I think everyone at one point has to face the fear of failure, especially if you have failed a lot in the past. Gain a different perspective of failure. Albert Einstein when asking about all the failed attempts at creating the light bulb simply said, "Those experiments were not failure but merely education. I learned from each failed attempt how to succeed." He kept experimenting until one he successfully created his invention.

2.   **Ignorance.** Many believe what you don't know can't hurt you. In the area of dreams, what you don't know can and will hurt you. Our enemy the devil seeks to keep you in the dark. The proverbial writer encourages us to pursue wisdom and knowledge. Ask God for wisdom and knowledge on how to fulfill your dream. You can stop the thief sent to steal your dream in its tracks with wisdom.

3.   **Rejection.** Rejection will attempt to destroy our dreams and aspirations. Jesus faced much rejection but probably none as painful as the rejection of his home town, family and friends. If rejection has sought to wipe out your dreams, take a moment to realize that through Jesus's death on the cross, the price paid for our sinful nature included rejection.

     Forgiveness is the only response to rejection. Embrace the spirit of adoption given to each of us when we were born again. Realize rejection has no place with us anymore, we can stop it at the door of our heart.

4.   **Offenses.** The trap and sin of offense is unforgiveness. Sin will cause us to detour from our assigned pathway of our dreams. Jesus warned us saying, "offenses will come to us all but woe to the ones offenses come through.

Realize we are all humans and make mistakes. We have all been hurt by someone or hurt another at one time or another. Decide to resist offense and forgive those our enemy sent to kill our dreams through offense.

5.   **Apathy.** Have you felt bored or indifferent about what you know you should be passionate about? Apathy can be subtle but deadly in its destruction of your dream. Ignoring apathy may lead us far off the path. Use apathy as a signal to check your heart.

Allow the Holy Spirit freedom to guide you and direct you in the way God wants you to go. Apathy sometimes can be an indicator that we moved past the Holy Spirit's gentle leadings to deal with hurt, anger or unforgiveness.

6.   **Weariness.** "I'm just tired of fighting! I give up!" Don't do that. The writer to the Galatians church knew the dangers of making decisions while you are weary. He encouraged the Church with, "Don't be weary in well doing for if you faint not, you will reap."

Begin afresh to take moments of rest and relaxation. Enter into the rest of God through faith. Remember the Sabbath. Don't ignore your body's call for rest. Turn aside to rest, you, your family and your work will be the better for it.

7.   **Lack of focus.** The Apostle Paul knew the power of focus saying, "This one thing I do…Lack of focus may steal the fulfillment of your dream. Not many days ago in a writers group, I listened to one of my friends saying, "I have so many unfinished writing projects that I feel I must finish something.

I encouraged her to focus on the project the Lord assigned her to last and let the others go. Don't let lack of focus cut in on your dreams and render you ineffective. Focus and finish the dream God gave you.

Our enemy Satan will sometimes try to use any or all of the above as a tactic through our own inattentiveness to our health and well-being. If you have been struggling with fear of failure, ignorance, rejection, offenses, apathy, weariness and lack of focus. Through Christ, you are equipped to overcome, so don't allow our enemy to push you into giving up or compromising your faith.

A Step toward Destiny

A Woman's Predestination

Teach us to number our days and recognize how few they are; help us to spend them as we should. —Psalm 91:12

The beginning journey of God's woman involves an exciting principle for it reveals God's heart for His women. It reveals a lovingly arranged destination (end result) for her that is good and full of purpose. It shows Father God wants us (His women) to have a deep awareness or sense of destiny operating in our lives.

He desires that we know His direction and plans for us so that we may get in agreement with Him. Consider this; how can we accomplish God's will and purpose for our lives if we don't know what it is or even that we have a happy ending reserved for us?

In today's society, many of us believe only those from a prominent or wealthy families have the edge needed for success in this life. Therefore, many of us base our value and self-worth on what family we were born into.

If we were fortunate enough to be born into a wealthy or prominently named family, we are worth a lot. But if we were unfortunate to be born into a family that lived in poverty and no prominence then we had very little value.

It is different in God's kingdom. We have been adopted into the family of God. It was his pleasure to prepare a wonderful future for each of us. A future filled with His good purpose and plans for our lives. God has given us a covenant promise. According to Romans 8:29 God has our destiny (final outcome) already set forth to be made into the image of His Son.

Even so, realistically knowing God has a happy ending reserved for us through Covenant promise of Jesus death, burial and resurrection. We also know that the enemy of God and His creation has a plan to steal, kill and destroy our dreams and destiny.

He will use circumstances, rejection, shame or sin designed to abort any desire to fulfill God's destiny in our lives. The devil's plans support his desire for us—an unexpected end, an unhappy ending and no chance to succeed.

With all that said, I propose it doesn't have to matter what the devil or anyone else has said about your life. Many times our enemy will speak over our lives through circumstances a destiny opposite what God has said.

Circumstances may rise up specifically designed to oppose the destiny of God in your life. You can gain a new life and sense of destiny from the Word of God. Remember, the words of the Prophet Jeremiah declaring God's heart, "For I know the plans I have for you…plans to prosper you and not to harm you, plans to give you hope and a future." (Jer. 29:11)

Take the Word of God put in your heart. Speak it out in faith and strengthen your sense of destiny. Your sense of destiny will affect how you look at everything. It will guide you to the very reason God put you on this earth. If you know what you are put on the earth to do, we can begin to fulfill God's purposes for our lives like never before.

Now is the time to know and connect with our destiny. Joan's awareness of her destiny gave her the sense of urgency needed to take the French soldiers to another level in a short time. There are some people that have that awareness of their future about them.

You just know they are fulfilling their God given purpose. Looking at the life of Joan and others who have fulfilled their God given destiny, there are some principles that will help us gain or develop that sense of destiny in our lives.

Recognize 'Now is the time. The main principle of gaining a sense of destiny is realizing that our time here on earth is brief. My prayer has become that of the Psalmist when he said, "Teach us to number our days and recognize how few they are; help us to spend them as we should. —Psalms 91:12

Seven Steps Faith Calls You To Take To Pursue Your Happy Ending

Realize the brevity of life. The Ecclesiastes writer describes our lives here on earth as a shuttle traveling swiftly through time or (psalms 78:39) Learn to number your days correctly. Jesus said to his disciples and now to us, "The day is almost ended, we must quickly fulfill our God-given task for night is coming, when no man can work."

With that said, the time is now to pursue, discover and fulfill our destiny, our appointed purpose here on earth. In this book, I've outlined seven steps to take in discovering your destiny. They helped me connect and find my destiny. I hope they will do the same for you.

1) **Go to your predestination.** Father God has lovingly planned in advance your good future, expected end and destiny. Like Cinderella, it has been hidden from your view for a season but now ready to be revealed…So, know you are on the journey to your predestined place.

2) **Pursue God's presence.** Let him give you His perspective. Ask God for His wisdom. All through the Bible inspired writers claim wisdom is the principal thing. Then listen a lot and pray more.

3) **Embrace the power of preparation.** There is a Kairos moment, even season in story for you. Knowing the power of preparation will keep you going through mistakes and fumbled decisions of life. This knowledge will cause you to view failure in a perspective that will cause you to get up and be strengthened instead of destroyed. You won't give in to languishing in self-pity. You will get up; brush yourself off and go at it again, becoming better not bitter.

4) **Stir the fires of your passion.** Raise your level of intensity. Stir up the gifts that lay within you to be used for God's glory. When you put these principles into action, you will learn how to truly turn the lemons of life into lemonade. You'll take those glasses of lemonade and serve them to the world.

5) **Discover your God-given individual purpose.** Find out what God put you on the earth to do. If you don't know, just ask. Ask and receive. Use God's phone number Jer. 33:3 Call unto me and I will show you great and mighty things…Then identify what seeks to make you ineffective.

6) **Experience the power of fulfilling your destiny.** Know your future, your destiny is stored in your heart. It's not dictated by your past or present circumstances.

7) **Run with prayer and perseverance** the race that is marked out for you. Be patient with yourself and others as you pray and walk out the will and purpose of God.

Finally, let us leave a legacy of mentorship. Are you preparing your life as a torch to pass on? Through this book and life lessons, the Holy Spirit has given me seven more steps outlined above that will move us toward fulfilling our passion, purpose and power in God. For more about the trilogy of WOW! Women books, visit our website http://wowontheweb.com

Strengthening Your Step

Go To Your Destiny

For He foreordained us (destined us), planned in love for us to be adopted (revealed) as His own children through Jesus Christ, in accordance with the purpose of His will—because it pleased Him and was His kind intent. — Ephesians 1:5b

We are surrounded by a cloud of witnesses. I see some familiar faces: Daddy, Grandma Minnie, Minnie Mama, Sam Daddy, Pappa-Peppers, Aunt Suge, Debra Texada and others who are still living their witness. Nevertheless, if I had to choose only one, I would choose my father, a farmer and a man of faith to share his example of faith and wisdom.

The event that would summarize his life of faith and allowing God to guide his actions would be the worst and longest drought season ever in Arkansas history. The ground had gotten so hard; there were deep long cracks everywhere. Everyone was getting worried. Many had already lost a lot of their crops. They had just dried up and withered away. My father kept saying if it did not rain soon we would most likely lose every crop.

Everyone was talking about irrigating from where ever they could. If we irrigated, ti would be from the man-made pond (dug to build Arkansas State Highway) down the road. My father and mother prayed about it knowing a few had already set up pumps. My father said God told him NOT to irrigate, it was going to rain. Some time went by and no rain. Everyone was irrigating full blast now. They were pumping water in from all over the place. They ridiculed my Dad but he kept saying we must wait on God if we irrigate now and then it rains we will lose everything.

Some more time went by and it began to rain. It rained and rained some more. Everyone that had irrigated lost their crops because the rain flooded it out. Our crops grew back looking better than ever. Even the truck patch gardening crops were beautiful. The corn stalks were the tallest and greenest we ever saw. They produced full ears of beautiful corn. The peas, cucumbers, sweet potatoes, everything was bumper.

In fact, they were some of the best crops ever. God certainly knew what He was talking about and so did my Dad. He was gracious and shared with all his surrounding neighbors even the ones that had ridiculed him the most. I learned; if you have a problem and you don't know what to do seek God. He'll show you what to do.

Your destiny or future is stored up in your heart! It's not dictated by your past or your current circumstances. Your destiny is determined by you. In the Scripture verse Matthew 12:34-35, "Out of the abundance of the heart the mouth speaks. A good man out of the good treasure of the heart brings forth good things: and an evil man out of the treasure brings forth evil things."

Jesus made this powerful statement to illustrate that what was in your heart is what comes out. Have you wondered: Who stored up the evil things in the evil man's heart? Clearly, the evil man himself did. Who stored up the good things in the good man's heart. Again, the man himself did.

In the same way, we are the only ones that can store and harvest the Word of God in our heart. Our parents can't store good in our hearts. Neither can our spouse. Your godly leaders can't do it. Even God can't do it for us. He has already done His part to help us.

He's the One Who made our heart to be a depository for His Word. He opened an account for us when we were first born. Our heart remains a depository whether it is for good or bad. We will use our faith for the good or for the bad.

The writer of Romans says, "God has dealt to every man the measure of faith." (Romans 12:3) The moment each of us made a decision to receive Christ, God put an initial measure of faith in our heart. Yet, we are the only ones that can increase that store.

We can increase our deposit of faith by taking the Word of God and putting it into our heart. Each time, we make a deposit of God's Word, our faith balance grows and our future and destiny get brighter. The more we deposit, the better things are, because that is where we will draw from to change the circumstances in our life.

Our heart holds the faith we'll need to combat any negative circumstances the devil sends our way. It doesn't matter if he tries to put sickness, rejection or troubles in our life to predict our end. We can draw from the Word of God about healing, acceptance or deliverance and it will give us victory in that area.

Crossroads

The Race Of Life

In the Gospels the Apostle Paul likened our life to a race," Therefore we also, since we are surrounded by so great a cloud of witnesses, let us lay aside every weight, and the sin which so easily ensnares us, and let us run with endurance the race that is set before us." —Hebrews 12:1, NKJV

In the race of life there is a contest of strength, survival, faith, wisdom and understanding. Most of all, we are joined by a great cloud of witnesses that have run the race before us.

No life run well is silent. (Hebrews 12:1 NKJV) Out of the advice, the writer of Hebrews gave the Christians there are three top principles that we may gain insight and life lessons for our own race set before us.

1. **Recognize** the cloud of witnesses around us. Who composes the cloud of witnesses? They are those that have gone before us or surround us now living a life of character that speaks today. The Bible mentioned those considered heroes in the hall of faith: Abraham, Joseph, Moses, Rahab among others who ran the race of life well.

2. **Lay aside** every hindrance and sin. The Hebrew writer's instructions to lay aside every hindrance and sin suggest a choice. That choice is to lay aside every interruption, distraction, trap, disappointment and delay designed to hinder us in our race of life. Additionally, the sin that easily ensnares us. Teach us to number our days and recognize how few they are; help us to spend them as we should. –Psalms 91:12.

3. **Run** the race set before us to obtain the prize. Live each day with the awareness that each day, month, year and life count. Do you not know that those who run in a race all runs, but one receives the prize? Run in such a way that you may obtain it. (I Co. 9:24, NKJV)

But there are still others that are more personal heroes and heroines to us. Review the cloud of those that have impacted your life with their character, their endurance or perhaps their joy.

In looking in your cloud and reviewing their lives, if you could choose one person and summarize one of the most important bits of wisdom gained from their life, who would that person be and what wisdom gained from them would you share with the world?

Spotlight

Five Stumbling Blocks To Avoid In The Race

I discovered that in any contest for a prize there will be obstacles—things that will rise up to hinder or resist you in your contest. Therefore, it's no surprise it's the same with life in general. Interruptions, distractions, obstacles may seek to stop us from receiving our prize (happy life, good and expected ending, heavenly home) But God has not left us to fight alone. What are some of the things that we should lay aside that may hinder us in our race of life?

1. **Half-heartedness.** Do you not know that those who run in a race all runs but one receives the prize? Therefore, run in such a way that you may obtain it.

2. **Complacency.** Que se-ra, se-ra. You know whatever will be, will be. Don't just lean back and accept whatever comes to you. Take life by the wheel and go after what you want.

3. **Prayerlessness.** You have not because you ask not. Jesus reminded us in the Gospels that, "Man ought to always pray and not give up."

4. **Impatience.** Quickly giving up. The Ecclesiastes writer supports this principle by saying the race is not given to the swift nor the skilled but the who perseveres.

5. **Sin.** Sin will stop us in our tracks, if we allow it. Our Lord Jesus has paid a great price for the opportunity we have to repent and make it right. Before His death, burial and resurrection we had a faulty access to the Father.

    Now, we can go boldly to His throne through Jesus and ask for forgiveness and receive it. So, don't let sin block your blessed life and your happy ending. Repent, receive and rejoice in the race!

You see God has lovingly arranged and designed your future. Has it emerged like a shining sun in your heart, yet? If not already, I pray it will soon. He, our Father, has arranged beforehand that we each would have our chance to succeed in the race of life. So take the advice offered from your cloud of witnesses, run your race well! Remember, we have a choice and a responsibility to lay aside every weight and the sin that so easily ensnares us.

Summary

Have you wanted your happy ending? The destiny seed of your future; God has put it in your heart, already. You didn't make it up. The seed that the Prophet Jeremiah proclaimed to Old Testament Jews and now to us is still the same: God has planned for, thoughtfully initiated, and even designed a blueprint for our future. —Jeremiah 29:11

I was amazed and elated to see that so much of God's heart and enthusiasm was revealed through the three small words of plan, hope and future through that Scripture. Remember, plan was defined as thoughts (not only thoughts but thoughtfulness and care), blueprint, direction or purpose.

Hope was explained as your expectancy of good, your faith, your dream, an expected good end (a happy ending) and even your destination. The definitive word future pointed to God's plan for our chance to succeed, our due season, our final outcome, our fate or simply our destiny.

So, we can say with confidence, God has a blueprint for my life. He has planned my destiny and I will receive my chance to succeed. I pray you were charged, as I was, with the knowledge that it is our responsibility to lay aside every weight and the sin that so easily besets us to run the race God has set before us.

I hope it was good news, as it was to me, to discover Father God's desire to give us a happy ending. Additionally, He wants us to have an awareness of our destiny that will cause every woman of God to turn to each other saying, "Now is the time! Go to your destiny!"

Destiny Challenge:

Go to your destiny! Put the WOW Women of Destiny logo on your website as a symbol of the star you are called to be. You are a star! God said so.

Chapter Two

Walking through the Process

A Woman's Pursuit Of God's Presence

You shall hide them in the secret place of Your presence. —Psalm 31:20a

What did Rahab, a former Jerichoian prostitute do that landed her in the Christian faith hall of fame, an honorable mention in the genealogy of Christ and changed her and her family's destiny forever? She was among those that trembled with fear at the mention of the Israelis' God, who fought for His people. Yet trembling with fear, Rahab grabbed her destiny and the fate of her family with both hands and did something that changed their lives forever.

She used her simple gift of hospitality to receive the Israelis spies and hid them when the King of Jericho sent men to get the strangers, after hearing they had arrived in the city. Rahab trusted a God she had only heard about; she made a pact with the Israelis Special Forces before sending them in the opposite direction of the King's men looking for them. It was all credited to her as righteousness.

Rahab's act of faith not only saved her entire family in a city that perished but set the pattern of simple faith by righteous actions for generations to come. Rahab was one of four women that received an honorable mention in the genealogy of Christ. From biblical history, we know that Rahab married Salmon, the father of Boaz and the great-great grandfather of King David.

By faith, the Israelites marched around the walls of Jericho for seven days, and the walls fell flat. By an act of faith, Rahab, the Jericho harlot, welcomed the spies and escaped the destruction that came on those who refused to trust God. (Joshua 1)

Sign Post To Destiny

Five Ways To Pursue God's Presence

Day by day I'll set you free more free than you ever thought you could be. –Father God

Have you felt disqualified from destiny because of your past? Rahab may have felt that way. She is a wonderful trophy of God's grace and merciful intent. Yet, she didn't start out that way. As you may know, her past included prostitution.

She pushed past her feelings of disqualification and made a declaration, "Your God is God." The first step toward realizing the destiny for God's woman is her pursuit of God's presence. I call it pursuing God's presence and not so much the gift. Here are five ways to pursue the presence of God.

1. Seek first the Kingdom of God. The Kingdom of God is not meat and drink nor the body. But is peace, joy, love and other fruits of the Spirit. Don't seek your destiny, seek Him and you will soon find your destiny (His desired end). Why? Because he will make sure you find it.

2. Seek him with all your heart. He has promised when we seek him with a whole heart we will surely find him. I have discovered in Scripture that He may be out of our sight. But he is never really far.

3. Seek humbly. The Psalmist writer encourages us with, "The Lord is good and glad to teach the proper path to all who go astray; he will teach the ways that are right and best to those who humbly turn to him.

Where is the man who reverences the Lord? God will teach him how to choose the best. (Psalm 25:8,9,12) In other words, seek God humbly and he will teach you how to choose your destiny.

4. Seek through meditating on God's Word. In defining the word meditation, we can see more clearly how to meditate on God's Word. Meditation means to ponder, think about a lot, and mutter under your breath.

In the first book of Joshua, God instructs Joshua (now us) how to have good success in everything he does. He says to meditate on His word day and night. So, it becomes clear to have good success, we will think about, ponder and mutter under our breath.

5. Seek continually. Seek the Lord and his strength, seek his face continually (I Chronicles 16:11). The Physician Luke admonishes us to, "Keep on asking and you will keep on getting; keep on looking and you will keep on finding; knock and the door will be opened. Everyone who asks, receives; all who seek, find; and the door is opened to everyone who knocks (Luke 11:9-10).

Continue the journey to your destiny. Seek God's presence first through seeking the kingdom of God, seek him with all your heart, seek him humbly, meditate the word of God and seek him continually.

A Step toward Destiny

Six Darts Sent To Divide Your Heart

Years ago, a ministry friend and I would carpool to the ministry site. When I would ride with her, I would literally have to put my feet on top of the things in the passenger side of her car. There was no condemnation toward her from me. I would just climb in like it wasn't there.

But one day the Holy Spirit said, "If she would clean up her car, I would heal her mind. She wouldn't have to take medication anymore." I later found out she was on medication for her mind.

I wish I could say I had the courage to say something. But I didn't say anything; I just prayed for her. I continued climbing in, like it wasn't there.

A couple of weeks later, I saw her; she had cleaned up her car. She excitedly told me she was off medication. I said, "What happened?" She said, "I knew I needed to do it but I couldn't quite focus in and do it.

One day, my mind cleared and I did it." I can only say it was all God. Besides what happened for my friend, I never forgot that principle about disorganization.

Jesus said, "Blessed are the pure in heart for they shall see God. To see God is to be an intimate friend. There's a scripture that says, "Friendship of God is reserved for those who reverence the Lord." So, here are those six darts to guard against in seeking God, wholeheartedly.

1. **Pride is an enemy of intimacy with God.** Back in the Garden of Eden, when Adam and Eve failed God and sin broke their fellowship. I suspect that was one of the things that hurt the most, their loss of intimacy with Father God. The couple knew no resistance until the event of their sin. The Bible plainly tells us God resists the proud.

2. **Duplicity leads to a divided heart.** Let no double minded man think he will receive anything from God. A double mind with the things of God will always hinder us. Many times, lack of focus boils down to a double mind. When I catch myself with a divided focus toward the destiny of God, I'll stop, repent and ask the Holy Spirit for right focus.

3. **Wrong motives work against our relationship** with God. A past jail ministry leader would always say about the inmates we were inviting to come to a church service our group hosted every Thursday night in a halfway house for men, don't worry about them coming with wrong motives. We've all had wrong motives (doing the right thing for the wrong reason) at one time or another.

Perhaps they are coming to look at the pretty girls on our team. The fact is when they get in the church service atmosphere with worship, the Holy Spirit can work with them and convict them of any sin and wrong motives. As He does with us all; he works with us to change our heart and motives (intentions).

4. **Disorganization can give place to the enemy**; for he thrives in disorder. God is a god of order. Just like in the little story I began, if we're there, steeped in clutter and disorganization and don't know how to get out of this pattern, you're in a good place. You know you need help and you know who can fix it. Practically, start with the small. Do that to completion. Then do the next step God shows you. How do I know? It's all started and finished in faith. Just do it and see what happens.

5. Worldly distractions can take many forms. Distractions can be anything good or bad that moves your attention away from the great that God has called us to do. Make sure your television time is not luring your heart away from God. I know this is not a popular topic but I must say this. Your seemingly innocent entertainment via T.V. shows with worldly values and agendas may become distractions and corrupt the good character you've built in your life. Simply put, remember bad company corrupts good character.

6. Fleshly activities that run rampant. Allowing the flesh (human nature) to rule. The Bible says the flesh is at enmity with God. If we allow the flesh to rule in our life, we eventually open the door to the enemy. By the flesh, I mean the natural man that wants to do everything it wants to do and at any time it wants to do it. For example, being led by your old nature you may choose to live an undisciplined life. You know overeating all the time, over-indulging, over-dosing on TV or any other distraction.

There's only one thing left to say, start small and start now. Father God will meet you wherever you are. It's a good thing, he doesn't require us to clean up ourselves and straighten up our mess before we come to Jesus. You can come to God just as you are. Let Jesus be Lord of your life, as well as, Savior.

Strengthening Your Step

Seven Powers To Walk (Through The Process) To Your Destiny

But we all, with unveiled face, beholding as in a mirror the glory of the Lord, are being transformed into the same image from glory to glory, just as by the Spirit of the Lord. -2 Cor. 3:18

Has God said to you lately, you're on your way to your destiny? You're going to the next level? If you're anything like me, you get all excited (as we should be) that you're going to the next level. You say praise God! I'm going to the next level.

I'm on my way to my destiny! We're shouting all over the place. Did you hear the word of God for me, "He says I'm going to the next level? He probably means, Next stop – your destiny!"

Well, it's true; we just quoted it from the scripture above from 2 Corinthians 3:18 the word of God says we go from faith to faith, glory to glory...

But usually, when we hear that (some of you older saints you know what I'm about to say) the journey has JUST begun. You may as well strap in, buckle up and get ready for the PROCESS.

What God in His mercy doesn't tell us that we're about to start the PROCESS before we get to the next level. He knows us in our humanity, our frailty in our earthly tents that we might not be ready to hear that. So he shows us that end step (the next level, our destiny, our destination) to get our eyes on the prize.

He may show you the top step of the staircase but not the whole stair case. He knows that with this glimpse of the prize, the promise, our destiny that we'll enter the joy of it and be strengthened. I believe that's what happened for our Lord Jesus.

Let's go there quickly, Hebrews 12:3 says the author and the finisher of our faith who for the joy that was set before Him endured the cross, despising the shame and has sat down at the right hand of the throne of God. Remember, the joy of the Lord is my strength. He knows we'll need the strength to make it through...

I noticed many of you are saying, 'The process didn't kill me." That's well and good. Praise God that we made it through the process. But I believe God is reaching for some people that are still in the process.

They haven't made it through yet. Even as I say that, the Holy Spirit reminds me that we go to many levels in life. So guess what, that means that as we progress, we go through many PROCESSES.

My goal is to encourage you at whatever point you are in the process. God is a God of the strong finish. He loves happy endings. He wants the end of your process to be a good one, one of victory. He wants us to receive the promise and walk in His promotion and the victory.

Therefore, He has given us seven powers to help us finish strong. They all start with a (P) so you can remember and finish well in every process you have to go through to get to your destiny:

1. The Power of God's Presence. You know some things are just worth repeating. So, I know we just discussed this earlier. Again, I encourage you to seek His presence. When you seek me with all your heart you will find me. Jer. 29:12; Moses knew the power of God's presence. Exodus 33:14 And he said, My presence will go with you and I give you rest.

(Another translation says I will give you rest and success.) To us, this translates to 'My presence will go with you and I will give you rest and destiny.' I love it! And of course, our chapter theme scripture supports us with, 'You shall hide them in the secret place of your presence.' --Psalm 31:20a

2. The Power of God's Preparation. (Read more about this in the next chapter.) Enter God's preparation. When we enter God's preparation, we receive His perspective. Furthermore, He may be calling you to some consecration time. I can say that with each new ministry level, God has called me to some consecrated and extra Bible reading, prayer and studying time. But let me add this, God's preparation is not just for His pastors and teachers.

Your process may not be all to do with your ministry. It may be a personal new level. He may be calling you to strengthen and fortify your personal life and time with Him.

Read with me, 2 Timothy 2:20, 21 But in a great house there are not only vessels of gold and silver, but also or wood and clay, some for honor and some for dishonor. Therefore, if anyone cleanses himself from the latter, he will be a vessel for honor sanctified and useful for the Master PREPARED for every good work.

3. The Power of God's Pruning. Yield to His pruning. Varn and I have always loved plants and flowers, especially Varn. One time he had a really good season of roses. We had neighbors and friends stopping by to look at those roses…At the end of that season, I came out and he had cut them all down to stubs. Not knowing about pruning, I asked him why he did that? Some of the stubs looked as if they would never come back. He explained he felt led to prune them back heavily for a better harvest.

To make a long story short, the Holy Spirit showed me us (you and me) in that season. Sometimes, we feel so sharply pruned that we wonder if it will kill us. I can testify; it won't kill you. God sees that you are doing well and he wants a stronger harvest. Know that the Master Gardener is in control; his pruning won't kill you.

But it will make you better and more fruitful. By the way, the next season for the roses Varn pruned were some of the most beautiful roses I've ever seen. They were cascading everywhere and producing gorgeous blooms. God used the rose bushes as our teachable moment.

Even so, I must warn you when we go through God's pruning, everyone may not understand. In fact, you may be misunderstood. Notice in John 15:2 Jesus said every branch that bears fruit He prunes...it didn't say every branch that stumbles, that has sin in their life. As some of our critics may try to say.... So you can know if you are being severely pruning, it may just mean you are doing well but God wants a STRONGER YOU and even more fruit.

4. The Power of God's Patience. Exercise God's patience. In Hebrews 10:36 For you have need of patience, so that after you have done the will of God, you may receive the promise. What will of God, you may ask? After you have served in faithfulness, after you have received the Word with gladness, after you sought his presence, after you have yielded to his preparation and pruning, then there's patience.

Can I tell you another story? Many times in my Christian walk, God has said wait. I can't say that I have always understood the why of wait. But I can tell you each time God asked me to wait, after a little time it becomes clear it has been well worth the wait.

5. The Power of God's Perseverance. Continue in God perseverance. In the Kingdom, it's all about character - becoming more like Jesus. You know the race is not given to the swift but to those who endure to the end...Sometimes in God's sovereignty there's endure in the word patience and it becomes perseverance. Because we continue into perseverance. In Heb. 6: 15 And so, after he had patiently endured, he obtained the promise. (speaking of Abraham) Simply put, don't give up; keep going there's a victory waiting for you on the other side of perseverance.

6. The Power of God's Promise. Inherit God's promise. God has designed an ending to this process. He's a finisher and he's given us the spirit of the finisher. He wants us to receive the promise. So, to every process there should be an ending. He's given us the spirit of the finisher. Heb. 6:12 That you do not become sluggish but imitate those who through faith and patience inherit the promise.

7. The Power of God's Promotion. Expect God's promotion. Wait! There's more after you have received the promise and walking therein. Yes, that's not all; after you have received the promise then comes God's promotion (Next Level.) We can expect God to move us into our next level. If you don't already know this principle, I must let you know.

And if you do, I remind you God is in charge of raising us up. The Hebrew writer encourages us with, "No discipline (process) seems pleasant at the time, but painful. Later on, however, it (process) produces a harvest of righteousness and peace (promotion) for those who have been trained by it.

Remember God has a purpose in each process we travel through. He works all things to the good of those who love him. He's working his will and his way in us as we go through the process.

There's a story that a pastor friend told us that sums up all of what we've talked about. It shows us God is in the process, working in and through us moving us to our next level. He said one day a man found a cocoon of a butterfly.

A small opening appeared. He sat and watched the butterfly for several hours as it struggled to squeeze its body through the tiny hole. Then it stopped, as if it couldn't go further.

So the man decided to help the butterfly. He took a pair of scissors and snipped off the remaining bits of cocoon. The butterfly emerged easily but it had a swollen body and shriveled wings.

The man continued to watch it, expecting that any minute the wings would enlarge and expand enough to support the body, neither happened! In fact, the butterfly spent the rest of its life crawling around. It was never able to fly.

What the man in his kindness and haste did not understand: The restricting cocoon and the struggle required by the butterfly to get through the opening was a way of forcing the fluid from the body into the wings so that it would be ready for flight once that was achieved.

Sometimes struggles are exactly what we need in our lives. Going through life with no obstacles would cripple us. We will not be as strong as we could have been and we would never fly.

You are destined for your next level in Christ. Don't stop now. Keep going to your destiny!

Crossroads

T.R.U.S.T. And Submitting To God's Process

By faith, the Israelites marched around the walls of Jericho for seven days, and the walls fell flat. 31 By an act of faith, Rahab, the Jericho harlot, welcomed the spies and escaped the destruction that came on those who refused to trust God.

Have you been asking God for a whale (big fish of a promise)? I know I have. If so, don't be surprised when He moves you out of the little pond (comfortable place), to enlarge your capacity to receive. Perhaps it's no news to you; I've discovered He cannot send a whale to our little pond. So guess what, we have to change. We have to change our mind, our heart and sometimes our place, position and perspective must change. I hear you that can be a lot of changing. But remember we are being changed to a better place.

For example, some of you (us) have been praying, Lord take me to the next level, increase me, bless me, enlarge my territory and even give me my destiny, right? Which, as you know, are not bad requests. The Word of God says our Father takes us from glory to glory and He wants to increase us, bless us, enlarge us and even gives us our destiny (bright future, our expected end.)

Here's the problem sometimes in response to our prayers change happens; then we get all confused. We start doubting ourselves and God's plan. God I prayed for increase. Why did I lose my job? I prayed that you enlarge me and now I'm in a battle. Consider this, God may be moving you from the little pond to the sea or even the ocean. Remember, whales don't swim in little ponds.

In the Bible, Joseph had to submit to the process. In perplexing circumstances, to say the least, he had great opportunity to doubt himself and God's plans. Even through the years, we don't see a record of Joseph trying to run off (get away from the process).

Instead, the Bible records he submitted to his masters and received the blessing and favor of God in the midst of whatever he was going through. In fact, Genesis 39:2 starts out with a description of Joseph that didn't sound like he was going through any process.

The Lord was with Joseph, and he was a successful man...

Then it said:

..and he was in the house of his master, the Egyptian.

Oh, so he still was going through the process. Don't worry; your next level may not take twenty years of process. Whatever it takes, know that the longer your process, the bigger the promise (next level) is going to be. God does not cut corners or waste our pain. He works all things to our good. (Romans 8:28)

Let me be clear, Father God is faithful. He will not fail us or forsake us. So here is our pattern to follow, we must submit to the process. Here are some suggestions formed into the acronym T.R.U.S.T. that will help us through the process.

Timing. First of all God's plan and timing is always perfect. (Ecclesiastes 3) Ours is not. It takes time to walk through the process. If we try to depend on just our sense of when things should be done, we may miss God.

If we pray and ask for His timing, we will have success. Operating in God's timing, we may have to wait and others times we must act when He says act.

Recompense: God will recompense. He always recompenses. The first time I heard the word recompense, I knew it was God speaking because that word was not in my vocabulary. If you hear nothing else I say in the chapter today, get this one in your spirit. Jehovah Gmolah is one of the names of God. Whatever losses you experience in the process; you can expect Father God will pay you back. He will restore.

For a little better understanding of God's recompense, let's define recompense. Recompense is to repay or reward or to compensate as in (loss, etc.) Prophet Jeremiah declares, "For the Lord is the God of recompense. He will surely repay." (Jer. 51:56)

Understanding. It's our human nature or fleshy nature, that we feel we have to always understand everything intellectually. It may not be to our best interest to know everything. For example, it's a known fact that many doctors and nurses can have a tough time believing in God's miraculous healing. Many say it's because intellectually they are trained to know all the tiny ways things can go wrong.

Or on the flip side, many scientists are becoming believers after much study and calculations proven about the earth and the universe. The result in their minds become, nothing this perfect and well-ordered can just come erupt out of chaos. (The Bang Theory)

Sovereign: God is in control. Say yes to His will. Acknowledge God is still God, even if we don't understand everything at the moment. Believe He has something bigger and better in mind. This is where the element of trust will enter, if we allow it. God is sovereign.

Territory: After God has moved you from your little pond, know that you are at the brink of your promise, your increase, your new level. But it's not time to relax; it's time to get ready to rumble (fight.) Not the way we're used to fighting. Get full of God's Word and fight the way He fights, by the Spirit. (2 Cor. 10:4) Pray more; listen more.

Get your plans, your strategies from God. He'll take you by the hand and help you. There are times you won't have to fight for the battle is the Lord's. There are other times you must fight the good fight of faith, using weapons that are not carnal but mighty to the pulling down of strongholds. (2 Cor. 10:4)

So, keep praying to God to bless you, increase you and enlarge your territory. He will. It's his good pleasure to do so. Just be ready for the conquest, taking dominion and occupying the good land he's given you. It takes pressure and sometimes pain to get you to the next level and into your destiny. Don't be dismayed and confused about what you're going through.

Ultimately, Jesus has given us the victory. The writer to the Corinthians said it like this, "Now thanks be to God who always leads us in triumph in Christ... (2 Corinthians 2:14) T.R.U.S.T God and know that He is in control. Listen to Him, follow Him, submit to the process and He'll get you to your destiny-ation, safely.

Spotlight

Do As Rahab Did

Have you wondered if your destiny in God matters in the large scheme of things? Really, have you wondered who cares? I can say without any doubt in my heart; God cares about your destiny.

Even if sowing your seeds of destiny have simply been handing a glass of water to the least of your brethren, your leaders, your flock or your family, it matters to God. 1

He cares so much he wants to reward you for it. What do you think of when you hear the word 'reward'? Many think of ministry gain, job promotion, monetary gains, etc.

And some even think of heavenly rewards. They all sound good; but it's really up to God about the rewards. I just know He rewards the righteous, his good and faithful servants.

But wait! Before you stop reading, I've learned a principle I want to share with you. That principle is: If you take care of God's family, His house, His business he'll take care of your family, your house and your business. He promises to be Jehovah Gmolah in your life if you sow your service into the Kingdom of God. Jehovah Gmolah is the Lord of Recompense, the One who pays you back. 2

You may remember King David and how he wanted to build God a house. But God told him he couldn't because he had become such a man of war to conquer the kingdoms God wanted him to. There was too much blood on his hands before the Lord. He went on to say he would allow his son Solomon to do it because he would be a man of peace.

Now, this is the part I want you to pay special attention to; God also told King David that he appreciated his heart so much to take care of His house that He would build him a house an everlasting house—a dynasty even. 3

Then there's Cornelius who was such a big giver into what is close to God's heart (the poor) that God sent an angel to help get Cornelius and his whole family saved. The Scripture describes him this way, "a devout man and one who feared God with his entire household, who gave alms generously to the people and prayed to God always." He operated in almsgiving so strong it had come up before the Lord as a memorial. 4

Father God has even proven this principle in my own life. Years ago, I was a new Christian. I know some of you can relate to this. I had such a burden for my family to be saved, delivered and walk in the fullness of God. But they wouldn't listen to me. Not one bit. So, I thought anyway.

You know how it can be; our family can be too acquainted with our past sins. Or they are just plain too familiar with us to hear the Word of God through us. Remember when Jesus (who was sinless) went back to Nazareth to minister to his village and neighborhood family. Skeptically, they were saying, "Isn't that Joseph and Mary's son? We know his brothers and sisters…"5

So this is where I was with my family and new commitment to God. No matter how hard I tried I was getting nowhere with them. Finally, I was on my knees crying before God about my family. Some of us as baby Christians can be so dramatic but sincere. Anyway, I was going on and on about it in prayer. Then I heard clearly from the Holy Spirit, "Do as Rahab did!"

Since, I was a baby Christian I didn't exactly know what Rahab did. I stopped my crying and got up to find out. To make a long story short, about forty years or so after God delivered the Israelites from slavery in Egypt, there was woman name Rahab who lived on the wall of a city called Jericho. God had given this city to the Israelites. They had to by faith conquer it and possess it.

Joshua, Moses assistant before he died was now leader of God's people. God had given him strategies to lead the people in conquering the city of Jericho. Joshua sent in spies to access the land and people. Rahab risked her safety and possibly her family's safety by helping the Israelite spies escape when the King heard they were there.

In return the Israelite spies made an agreement with her for helping them. When they returned to take the land they would spare her and her family if she had them with her in one specific place. Well, the Word of God says Rahab was there and her entire family; they were all spared as the Israelites took the city. Bible historians report she married one of the spies which is how she ended up in the genealogy of Christ.6

I don't know how your mind works; but when I read that I immediately begin to gain respect for Rahab. If your family is anything like mine, they can be pretty stubborn at times. So how did she get her whole family to be in one place at the same time?

From the story, Rahab may not have been the most respected person in the family. She was said to be a prostitute; so her past may not have spoken well of her. Nevertheless, she had them all in one place when the spies arrived. So none was lost; that statement alone made me want to do what Rahab did. I too wanted none to be lost in my family. 7

After thinking about this story awhile, I realized what Rahab did was use her faith in God. She followed his instructions through the spies. Her part was to receive the men of God in peace and help them gain access to the information they needed.

And her part was to help them escape when the time came. In a similar way, our part is to help the House of God wherever God has called us. And stay attentive for his instructions or promptings when an opportunity comes to influence our family.

Father God made an agreement with me that day. That agreement was if I would continue to help His family (the family of God) leading them to Christ, helping them get delivered and healed. He said if I would continue to serve in His house, he would take care of my family, my house, my business.

God has been faithful. I didn't always see it happen when I thought it should happen. But, I stayed faithful to His call. Now I can say, He has been faithfully saving, delivering and planting my family in His kingdom. Sometimes, he sends them to me to minister to and other times he sends other godly laborers in their path. Either way it's someone they'll listen to at the time.

I realize God used that simple little analogy to stir my faith. I hope it stirred yours too. Not only that, I believe God has the same covenant with all Christians. Remember, the Psalmist encouraged us with, "God abundantly blesses his faithful people."8

I can hear someone saying, "What about me I just started? I haven't quite achieved faithfulness in my service yet." That's no reason to be left out. Come on up; there's room at the table for you. In God's kingdom the last are first. I was just reading the parable when Jesus told the story about the Vineyard and its owner. The owner went out to look for day laborers three different times and hired people.

His third time out at almost the close of the day, he still hired a few workers. At the end of the day, he paid them all the same, one denarii. The ones that were hired at the beginning of the day got upset that the owner paid the last the same. In God's kingdom, He doesn't penalize you for the order you came. Even if you're a part of the latter, He gives each of us the fullness of His grace when we receive Him.9

So I encourage you, if you've been taking care of God's house and His business, you can get in expectancy. God's going to take care of your house, your family, your job or business. No worries; the global economy may be in recession. But your seeds of service have already been planted. The price has already been paid. Jesus paid the price on a hill call Calvary. That's why we celebrate Easter; He has risen!

It's in the receiving now. The Holy Ghost has already been sent. Salvation has come. Healing has already been paid for. What about prosperity? It's paid for too. So, get ready to receive by faith whatever you need. Your family, your house and your work is blessed because of YOUR seeds of service in God's Kingdom!

Summary

Are you weary with waiting for your destiny to appear? You have been looking for your moment to arrive. Well, I have good news! It's finally your time. God's words are no longer postponed or delayed. But the words He speaks are done.

All you have to do is receive it by faith. Now, you're eligible to join your faith with patience and receive the promise of God. Just like Rahab, a former Jerichoian prostitute, we have to take a step, a first step or a next step. You might be scared or you may feel a sudden peace.

Either way, now is the time. Look what happened for Rahab and others like her, including me. Her first step started the journey to her destiny. Eventually, it landed her in the Christian faith hall of fame, married to one of the spies, an honorable mention in the genealogy of Christ and changed her family's life forever?

And for me, to God be glory, I took my small gift of writing and multiplied it to twelve plus books, still counting, our publishing company and training service for experts, entrepreneurs, aspiring authors and especially WOW! Women.

Back to Rahab, the king and the whole city trembled in fear at news of the plans of the Israelis and their God. But Rahab alone confessed and believed, "Your God is God!" She stepped out and pursued God to save her entire family. And you know the story by now. God did it. He's doing it for me. And he will do it for you. See you next chapter, 'Seizing Your Season.' We've started the journey…

Destiny Challenge

Tell a story of a Sunday afternoon drive to picnic at a local park. The point is when you are going to a certain place, your destination. You don't take your foot off the gas pedal until you arrive. You keep propelling with your foot on the gas pedal, in effect driving the car, until you get there.

Chapter Three

Seizing Your Season

A Woman's Propitious Power of Preparation

But in a great house there are not only vessels of gold and silver, but also or wood and clay, some for honor and some for dishonor. Therefore, if anyone cleanses himself from the latter, he will be a vessel for honor sanctified and useful for the Master PREPARED for every good work. —2 Timothy 2:20, 21

W hen I was a young girl, still playing with dolls, a life-sized doll came on the market. My cousin and I had to have one. So, guess what we got for Christmas. We both received the most beautiful life-sized dolls we had ever seen. We would often pretend they had a change of clothes for a party.

In our favorite pretend-world, we would take the clothing off and pretend to put on evening gowns for a party. Of course in our mind's eye they had on the most beautiful evening gowns ever. I imagined an emerald green dress, form fitting, no sleeves with a trail while my cousin had on a flashy red one with ruffles.

We were girly-girls; so we didn't play outside much. This particular day, my mother had told us to go outside and play for she needed to do something in the area we were playing in.

In front of my folk's house was a highway and on the side was a dusty one lane road. We went outside and setup our imaginary dressing room on the side of the house.

We undressed the dolls and began putting on their imaginary gowns. We were having so much fun; we didn't notice any of the cars go by or that they were honking their horns. Later on, just as we were walking out of our imaginary door to go to the party, my mother came to the door and shouted, "Put the clothes back on those dolls and come inside!" We discovered she had received several calls from our neighbors and passersby asking if she knew the little White girls we were playing with outside were naked.

I told this story simply to grab your attention and gently prod you to thinking about preparation in your life. For when we are unprepared we are often as naked in our life, as the dolls I described just now.

Are you preparing for the opportunities in your future? Are you in expectancy of a Kairos moment? Many times, we are as unaware of the opportunities going by us as my cousin and I were of our neighbors going by honking their horns.

Sign Post to Destiny

Ready For A Kairos Season?

Success happens when preparation turns into readiness and runs into opportunity. —Earma Brown

An eclectic group of twelve people were looking for their Kairos moment. What virtue did they all commonly need to obtain it? Five out of the ten women used its power; so did Michael Jordan and Thomas Edison. What kept Jordan going through the failed baskets he made to perfect his game?

How did Edison continue in the face of countless botched experiments to gain a successful invention? And why did only five women enter in when the other five were left out with nothing to show for their effort? Seven of twelve used the precocious power of preparation.

So, are you ready for your Kairos moment? You might be wondering what Kairos means in general? So glad you asked! Kairos originates from the Greek language. It literally means opportunity; a propitious moment for decision or action.

To expand our thinking on the Kairos moment, *propitious* is giving or indicating a good chance of success; favorable; sign of good success; heaven-sent, providential. With all that said, we can look at a Kairos moment in Christ as being a heaven-sent opportunity; God timed season, decision or action.

In the story of Jesus about the ten virgin women, what virtue sought to ready all twelve people for their Kairos moment? Five out of the ten women knew its power; so did Michael Jordan and Thomas Edison. I mean, really, what kept Jordan going through the failed baskets he made to perfect his game? How did Edison continue in the face of countless botched experiments to gain a successful invention? And why did only five women enter in when the other five were left out with nothing to show for their effort? Here's the secret, in plain sight, seven of them used the power of preparation.

Jesus told a story about ten women and the power of preparation. Five of the ten women used it when getting ready to meet the Bridegroom. The story goes like this, "Then the kingdom of heaven will be comparable to ten virgins, who took their lamps and went out to meet the bridegroom. 2"Five of them were foolish, and five were prudent. 3"For when the foolish took their lamps, they took no oil with them, but the prudent took oil in flasks along with their lamps.

Now while the bridegroom was delaying, they all got drowsy and began to sleep but at midnight there was a shout, 'Behold, the bridegroom! Come out to meet him. Then all those virgins rose and trimmed their lamps. 8"The foolish said to the prudent, 'Give us some of your oil, for our lamps are going out.' 9"But the prudent answered, 'No, there will not be enough for us and you too; go instead to the dealers and buy some for yourselves.

And while they were going away to make the purchase, the bridegroom came, and those who were ready went in with him to the wedding feast; and the door was shut.

But he answered, 'Truly I say to you, I do not know you.' 13"Be on the alert then, for you do not know the day nor the hour. But he answered, 'Truly I say to you, I do not know you.' "Be on the alert then, for you do not know the day nor the hour."

The five of the ten women in Jesus' story were wise and prudent. They wisely prepared for the journey with extra oil. In the spirit of readiness, they armed themselves with a no, when their less wise sisters wanted them to share their oil with them.

I'm sure, they heard, 'what kind of Christian sister are you that you won't share?' Yet, they didn't share and stayed fully prepared to enter in their own destiny. They discovered this time, it wasn't about selfishness but obedience to stay prepared.

While in your season of preparation, know that God's timing is perfect. In his time (season) he makes everything perfect. In my immaturity, I've yielded to impatience or running ahead more times than I care to admit. Father God has taught me about his timing more and more over the years.

In Jesus story about the ten women in the wedding party waiting for the bridegroom to come and get them to usher them into the wedding, five of the women procrastinated about their oil and readiness to go, when he got there.

In fact, to show how important this virtue is or the lack of it, the five procrastinators missed their opportunity to enter in their purpose and even were rebuked for their carelessness in waiting. In a similar way, inside the kingdom of God, there are strategic 'God moments' that he will prepare us for. We have to become ready, stay ready and not yield to procrastination.

Thomas Edison is another example of a person who used preparation to enter his destiny. He developed his inventions by trial and error. Viewing his experiments as preparation, he described each so called failure as a learning opportunity for how his pending invention did not work.

Maybe the next trial would be the successful one; so he kept trying. He used the Law of Average. The Law of Average says for every ten things you try, seven to eight of them won't work. But the eighth or ninth time you try one of them will be successful.

So, the point of the story is to keep trying and keep waiting for your Kairos moment. You are bound to discover the winning combination. Mr. Edison sure did. He may be as famous for all the tries he did to accomplish his invention as he is with the eventual success.

Another great example, is Michael Jordan who didn't look at how many failed baskets he made? He only looked at increasing the successful baskets. In his endeavor to be the best, he didn't count the failed hundreds; he counted only the successful. Through his perseverance, he became one of the best and most celebrated basketball players in the history of professional basketball game.

A Step toward Destiny

21 Ways To Walk In The Spirit Of Readiness!

For I am the Lord, I do not change; --Malachi 3:6a

Have you noticed during these turbulent times a lot of things we thought would never change are changing? I drove by one of our favorite restaurants not long ago and noticed a sign "CLOSED After 50 Years." We had to start limiting our visits because of health reasons anyway but they still had a special place in our hearts and minds. You'll know why when I tell you what they were dishing out. They served some of the best fried chicken, I think, in the world. But things changed and they're gone.

Perhaps, you are in the midst of a change that you never thought would happen. If so, this little word is for you today. I encourage you to call to the one who changes not. Our Father God does not change. In fact, he is the same yesterday, today and forever. He promised he would never leave us or forsake us. And you know what; I believe Him. On that note, I've gathered some Scriptures that I have found comforting and faith building in the middle of CHANGES in my life and all around me.

o   Blessed be the Lord my Rock, who trains my hands for war, And my fingers for battle--My Lovingkindness and my fortress, My high tower and my deliverer, My Shield and the One in whom I take refuge. --Psalm 144:1,2a

o   "For I am the Lord, I do not change; --Malachi 3:6a

o Let your conduct be without covetousness; be content with such things as you have. For He Himself has said, "I will never leave you nor forsake you." So we may boldly say: "The Lord is my helper; I will not fear. What can man do to me?"

o "God is not a man, that He should lie. Nor a son of man, that He should repent. Has He said and will He not do? Or has He spoken and will He not make it good? --Numbers 23:19

With all that said, if God has given you a promise and the circumstances are saying different or even the opposite, find you a quiet place and begin to think on the things that He has already done. Stir up a grateful spirit (attitude.) Then begin to fill your heart and mind with Scripture that God always does what He says.

It may not be exactly like you thought. It may not even be when you thought. But God never fails. He always comes through for us. This may seem like a simple little exercise. And it is; but remember our weapons of warfare are not carnal but mighty in pulling down the strongholds of the enemy. (2 Corinthians 10:4)

Come on; let's continue to call on the One who changes not. Now, here are some things that will help us be ready for any opportunity.

1. **Allow God to take you the long way.** He often does this to purge us, prepare us, and ready us for victories and opportunities in our future.

2. **Don't despise small beginnings.** Learn to take life step by step. God designs increments in our lives. He often guides us step by step, level by level as we climb the staircase to our destiny.

3. **Gain knowledge.** Educate yourself. Take a class. Sign up for mentorship or coaching in your area or industry. The word of God says, "An intelligent man loves new ideas. In fact, he looks for them."

4. **Nurture creativity.** Remain up-to-date in your field. Look at what others are doing. Sow a seed. Invest in someone else's work. Surround yourself with related subject matter.

5. **Manage your dream.** Break it up into small projects or goals. Now, just do it. You can be sure; you are ready when opportunity knocks.

6. **Be diligent.** Have you developed your work ethics? For many of us, our work ethics were developed as a child or a young teen-ager. If not, now is a good time to get started. Just keep learning excellence as a habit.

7. **Allow time to develop your gifts and talents.** Even your anointing needs development on how to operate in it. Most of us weren't born genius. But any gift can reach near genius status, if developed.

8. **Prioritize your family, business and life.** Make sure God is first, family, work, church and then other stuff. Right priorities will safeguard your life. Most sin happens when something is out of balance with wrong priorities. For example, if you're putting work or church before God and family. Keep right priorities and prosper beyond your wildest dreams.

9. **Learn early to redeem your time.** Look for lost time (unredeemed) evenings, early mornings, late nights. In other words, if you're spending all your free time in front of television, you might not connect with your destiny in your life time.

10. **Apply patience.** The word of says to exercise patience so that afterwards you may receive the promises of God. Notice there's action inside this instruction. Most people think of patience in the noun or passive form. But, I've discovered it's more of an action, a verb.

11. **Do as Jesus did.** Jesus wrapped himself in a towel preparing to serve his disciples and impart the vision of servanthood in their hearts. By allowing Him to serve them, they learned a lesson they would never forget. To serve Jesus, effectively, we must serve each other. Ultimately, to love Jesus, effectively, we must love each other.

12. **Embrace your season of preparation.** Life really is cyclical. It comes around in season. You may be going through a season where it looks like nothing is happening. It may be your preparation season for the greatness that's coming. Take advantage of it; don't waste it.

13. Recognize prayer is a part of your preparation. Petition Father God with your request to know and walk in your destiny and purpose. Use his phone number, I told you about in an earlier chapter. You might remember, its Jeremiah 33:3 Ask me and I will tell you remarkable secrets you do not know about things to come.

14. Write it down. When Father God speaks to you about your future, your destiny, write it down. Make record of it, not just remembering it. It helps let our heavenly Father know you are serious about receiving it in faith. It not only helps him know but it helps your psyche and the whole universe that you are serious about your destiny. As Henry Ford said so eloquently, after a commitment is made all of heaven gets involved with help to bring it to pass. So, write it down.

15. Develop a spirit of readiness. To develop a spirit of readiness, you have to make a commitment to act. Set a date and find out why. Develop your skills and do the hardest first. Work on prudence. Announce your goal to someone or even publicly. You'll work harder to complete it. Your focus will automatically become purer. (See the Destiny Spotlight for more.)

16. Persistence. Did you make a goofy mistake at one point, don't give up? Thomas Edison failed thousands of times with the invention of the light bulb. Yet, he did not call it failure, he called it education. He was determined to learn from each test gone awry.

17. Take risk. Practice saying yes more. Try new things. Don't get stuck in doing the same old things and expecting a new result. That's insanity. You have to do things differently to experience a new result. Even, if it's a tweak here or there, do it. Shake it up. Do it a little bit different. You might be surprised at the difference!

18. Work hard at preparing. The Word of God says, King David prepared with all his might to build the Temple of God. Don't do it half-hearted. If it doesn't move you, it probably won't move anybody else, not to mention God. Another good example is, "The effectual, fervent prayer of a righteous man avails much."

19. Trust God. Realize God is trustworthy. He won't disappoint you. The psalmist declared, "But I trust in you, O Lord I say, 'You are my God.' My times are in your hands . . ." –Psalm 31:14, 15

20. Endure hardship. You know, we all go through something. More importantly, it may not all be over when we want it to. The writer of 2 Timothy said, "Endure hardship as a good soldier." Don't despise the Job factor in your life or anyone else's life. Since you're God's child, know that He is still in control. And He disciplines his kids. Mr. Lewis said it like this. "Hardships often prepare ordinary people for an extraordinary destiny." -O.S. Lewis

21. Stay prepared. Before anything else, preparation is the key to success. -Alexander Graham Bell Ladies and Gentlemen, I can only add to that, stay prepared with faith and patience until your promise arrives. Right before my faith was rewarded with my husband Varn, the Holy Spirit kept prompting me stay ready, Earma, stay ready. Your promise is imminent...Then one day, twenty-three years ago, God sent Varn into my life. I can truly say when God asks you to wait, it is worth the wait...

With all that said, staying ready doesn't mean things will never change. Being ready may just mean staying ready to change, holding on lightly to the things of this world. And cultivating a mind and heart ready to go with Jesus when He comes again. Or even, just as importantly, staying ready to obey when He leads, prompts and directs you.

Strengthening Your Step

Carpe Diem! 10 Ways To Seize The Season

There is a season for every activity under heaven. –Eccl. 3:1b

Do you know what season your life is in? Are you in the preparation season? Or are you living your dream and destiny? For many the preparation season is spent preparing for a destiny to come. For others, it might be going through the process.

God has communicated to you; the next level or the promise is coming. You might know by now, that means the process is about to happen which readies you for the next level. For He only shows a few steps of the staircase at a time.

Whatever season, this message finds you in, you should maximize it. Live it to the fullest. Many times, over the years, I found myself mourning over a past season or spending too much time wishing for the next season. Instead, I've learned to live fully in my present season, yet remain expectant for the upcoming season.

The word maximize means to assign maximum importance to; to find a maximum value of; the period of highest, greatest or utmost development (plain terms: to give the best of all that you have to God and to receive all that God has for you in your present season.)

1. Recognize and know YOUR season. —Ecclesiastes 3:1

2. Interpret the signs of the God-ordained season. —Matthew 16:2, 3

3. Decide to use your gifts and talents for God. —Matthew 25:14-30

4. Make your calling and election sure.   —2 Peter 1:3-10

5. Live a balanced life. —Luke 2:52, 2 Timothy 1:7

6. Build a prayer life with God. —John 15:1-7

7. Set up a consistent Bible reading program. —Luke 6:48

8. Learn to listen to the Holy Spirit. —Romans 8:14

9. Live a fasted life style. —Matthew 6:16-18

10. Live ready. —I Timothy 4:2; Matthew 25:1-13

11. Encourage others in their season. —Hebrews 10:23, 24, 25

According to the writer of Hebrews 10:23, 24, 25, Let us hold unswervingly to the hope we profess, for he who promised is faithful. And let us consider how we may spur one another on toward love and good deeds.

Let us not give up meeting together, as some are in the habit of doing, but let us encourage one another—all the more as you see the Day approaching.

So, are you ready? Ready for God's purpose and plan to come forth in your life. Ready for the fulfillment of God's Word in your life. Ready for God's opportunities, his ordained Kairos moments. Ready to connect with your destiny. Ready to be about our Father's business. Ready for the Second Coming of our Lord!

There really is a season for everything. The wise writer of Ecclesiastes 3:1 There is a time for everything, and a season for every activity under heaven. Jesus said we can know the season, we are experiencing. In fact, he expects us to know the season, led by the Holy Spirit.

For if we stay in step with the Holy Spirit, he will prompt us on what season, we're living. And, I might add, show us how to take full advantage of our present season and the ones coming up. For there might be some SUDDENLIES along the way.

The writer of Matthew 16:2, 3 He replied, "When evening comes, you say, 'It will be fair weather, for the sky is red, 3 and in the morning, 'Today it will be stormy, for the sky is red and overcast.' You know how to interpret the appearance of the sky, but you cannot interpret the signs of the times . .

With all that said, we know we will experience different seasons at different times in our life. As we stay connected and led by God's Spirit, we can discern and know the seasons of life.

In this chapter, we have been discussing our preparation season and how we can operate in a spirit of readiness and stay ready for God's opportunity and destiny.

Crossroads

Guarding Against The Five Top Enemies To Readiness

As with any virtue of Christ, there are always enemies, sent to make us unready. Or we are lulled to sleep by the cares of this world, deceitfulness of riches and more. Here are few things to watch out for from the story of the ten virgins.

Then the kingdom of heaven will be comparable to ten virgins, who took their lamps and went out to meet the bridegroom. 2"Five of them were foolish, and five were prudent. 3"For when the foolish took their lamps, they took no oil with them, but the prudent took oil in flasks along with their lamps.

Now while the bridegroom was delaying, they all got drowsy and began to sleep but at midnight there was a shout, 'Behold, the bridegroom! Come out to meet him. Then all those virgins rose and trimmed their lamps. 8"The foolish said to the prudent, 'Give us some of your oil, for our lamps are going out.' 9"But the prudent answered, 'No, there will not be enough for us and you too; go instead to the dealers and buy some for yourselves.

And while they were going away to make the purchase, the bridegroom came, and those who were ready went in with him to the wedding feast; and the door was shut. But he answered, 'Truly I say to you, I do not know you.' 13"Be on the alert then, for you do not know the day nor the hour. But he answered, 'Truly I say to you, I do not know you.' "Be on the alert then, for you do not know the day nor the hour.

The story of the 'Ten Virgins' has a double reference in its meaning and interpretation. We know, Jesus was referring to his Second Coming. But it, also, can apply to being alert, ready and even prepared for God's destiny and opportunity. With that in mind, here's five top enemies to the spirit of readiness for God's destiny.

1. **Procrastination.** Procrastination is an enemy to readiness. By nature, we seem to delay doing what we know to do. Then before we know it, it's the last minute. Like the five virgins, the hour arrives without notice.

2. Misunderstanding. Jesus said to some of his followers and now us through the Bible, we can discern the weather accurately, yet we fail to discern the season, we're living in. Are you in a season of preparation?

If so, cooperate and yield to the Holy Spirit's promptings to ready yourself for the plan of God. Then, there are those who are ready. You are in the waiting wings of life. You have need of patience so that after you have done the will of God, you may inherit the promise of God.

3. Distractions. Five of the women were called foolish or lacking judgement. In modern language, I would say they failed to use common sense. It's not like they had to be a rocket scientist to know to bring extra oil.

Maybe, they were distracted. At any rate, our world is much more fast paced than in the times, Jesus lived and told this story. So, I would say we need to guard against distractions of our age.

4. Worldliness. In James 1:27, the writer describes what Father God considers as religion, "Pure and undefiled religion in the sight of our God and Father is this: to visit orphans and widows in their distress, and to keep oneself unpolluted by the world. So, one of the enemies to readiness is worldliness, being more like the world and its sinful ways than not.

5. Disobedience. We must keep a heart that's ready to repent of any sin, willful or unknown. By that I mean, when the Holy Spirit shows us something, we didn't know, we repent.

By the Holy Spirit's guidance, we can all become one of the wise women who are ready. We can diligently guard against the enemies of faith and readiness and stay ready for the destiny of God and the Second Coming of our Lord Jesus Christ.

Spotlight

The Five Powers of Patience

For you have need of patience so that after you have done the will of God you may receive the promise. –Hebrews 10:36

Patience is a highly under-rated virtue. Most people look at patience as the virtue everyone needs but no one wants. Our society does not promote patience. Most things are geared toward right now, immediately and instantly. The farmer knows the power of patience. For if he did not have patience after his crop is in the ground, he would go out and pull his plants up by the root to see what stage of development it's in; thereby destroying the growing plants.

1.   **Get on God's timetable.** Know that he makes everything beautiful in its time. His timing is perfect.

2.   **Do the will of God.** After you have done the will of God, use your patience so that you may receive the promises of God.

3.   **Work your muscle of patience.** When we work the muscle (virtue) of patience it gets stronger and stronger. Until, finally one day it is perfect. You may know this but perfect as Christians means mature.

4.   **Release the power of patience.** Just knowing you need patience is not quite the same thing as exercising patience. You have to release the power of patience by exercising that muscle. You can exercise it by confessing, "I'm patient. God's timing is perfect. He is in control of my life." Then allow your actions to line of with what you just said.

5.   **Know that with faith and patience** you inherit the promises of God. Use the law of double portion, when something is combined with another thing, it is automatically more powerful. Join your faith with patience and receive the promise of God. Make a commitment to act. Set a date. Find out why. Develop your skills. Do the hardest first. Develop prudence.

Announce your goal to someone or even publicly. Trust me; you'll work harder to accomplish it. Your focus will automatically become purer. Know that using patience, you are indeed developing a spirit of readiness. You will be like all the other Saints of God in the Bible and in our modern day, you will receive the promise through faith AND patience.

Summary

Are you ready for your Kairos season? Or are you as unprepared as the life-sized dolls, I described in my introduction. I learned working with the Holy Spirit, we each can be ready for our God timed season of success. To get started, get organized and develop a spirit of readiness. Simply put, it's get ready and stay ready. You may be like I was, the Holy Spirit is now prompting you stay ready, precious one, stay ready. Your promise is imminent...

I was reminded that the promises are received through faith and patience. We receive what we believe now. But just like the ten virgins who awaited the Bridegroom, we await the promises of God to manifest and materialize in our lives.

As we stay connected and led by God's Spirit, we can discern and know the seasons of life. In this chapter, we have been discussing our preparation season and how we can operate in a spirit of readiness and stay ready for God's Kairos opportunity and destiny.

Remember when you use patience, you are indeed developing a spirit of readiness. You will become like all the other Saints of God in the Bible and in our modern day, you will receive the promise through faith and patience.

With all that said, staying ready doesn't mean things will never change. Being ready may just mean staying ready to change, holding on lightly to the things of this world. And cultivating a mind and heart ready to go with Jesus when He comes again. Or even, just as importantly, staying ready to obey when He leads, prompts and directs you to your Kairos season and even your destiny.

See you next chapter, we discuss 'Turning Our Troubles Into Triumph'. We're on the DESTINY journey...

Destiny Challenge

Symbolic Illustration: Get a pack of Eveready batteries. Tell the story logo of the pink drum beating rabbit that keeps going and going. Or use Jesus' story of the ten virgins and substitute lamps with batteries.

Chapter Four

Turning Your Troubles Into Triumph

A Woman's Fiery Passion Points To Purpose

No one lights a candle and puts it under a bushel. —Matthew 26:10

Candi Lightner was considered a normal housewife with children. So what caused this housewife to almost single handedly change the nation of America's complacent thinking about drinking while driving? On May 3, 1980 her twelve-year-old daughter, Cari was killed by a drunk driver.

This unexpected and tragic event changed the course of Candy's life. In the middle of the grief of losing a teen-aged daughter, Ms. Lightner made a promise not to let this tragedy and others like it go unnoticed.

Only four days later, Candy met with some of her friends to discuss what they could do to make an impact on drunken-driving fatalities. Armed with a passion to help other mothers face similar tragedies, she formed MADD (Mothers Against Drunk Driving) and in the process turned her troubles into triumphs.

Have you suffered a setback, a disappointment, even a tragedy? Then know you are a candidate like no one else to discover your passion. You can know that God did not cause the evil in your life.

But he has promised to work all things to the GOOD of us because we love Him and are called according to His purpose (Romans 8:28). If the devil has initiated some setback, disappointment or trouble in your life, decide with me to give him a black eye, seek the Lord and discover your passion!

When Jesus walked this earth he had a passion for helping God's people and destroying the works of Satan. Indeed, Scripture says, "For this purpose was the Son of God made manifest."

His passion led him to his purpose and destiny (1 John 3:8). Ms. Ligntner is passionate about never letting what happened to her daughter happen to another family. Discover your passion it may lead you to your purpose!

Signpost to Destiny

What Lights The Fire In Your Eyes?

There is nothing quite as exhilarating as getting out of bed in the morning, going back into the world, and knowing why. Enthusiasm is derived from the certainty that for this I was born, and I am doing it! It is thrilling knowledge that I am fulfilling God's intended purpose for me. —Bill Hull

Have you ever found yourself passionless, listless, and bored to tears with life? I did. During that time someone asked me, "Do you ever get excited about anything?" It hurt me because I knew this person was sarcastically implying I was a boring person leading a boring life.

Nevertheless, it triggered my thinking. I began to ask myself some hard questions about why I felt so emotionally void. Why was there no sparkle in my eyes? Was I getting a charge out of anything in my life or did I just exist from day to day.

After examining myself, I was discouraged with what I saw. While mulling it over in my mind one day my Lord spoke to me through His talent story. I read the story and began to feel convicted about not using my talents. I looked back over my life and took inventory of my decisions. I could clearly point to only two choices that were not compromise or settling for the easy route.

I repented to God for not using what he had given me to use. I began tracing my life back to some passions I had as a child. I loved to write and read. I remembered devouring book after book from the moment I learned to read at five. I was secretly happy when my mother would send me to my room as punishment because there I could enter another world through books.

God has given each person a unique gift or set of gifts. In the Jesus' talent story the owner gave each person a different number of talents. From this we may realize, God has given some numerous gifts while others he has given a couple or even one.

What prompted my passion search was the fact that no matter how many he had given to any person, he expected it to be multiplied when he came back. You may have to go back to early childhood to re-discover your passion. What have you always enjoyed doing since as far back as you can remember? What has always gotten you stirred up? What used to light the fire in your eyes?

A Step toward Destiny

Lit For A Purpose

No one lights a candle and puts it under a bushel. Matthew 26:10

Candi Lightner and a group of mission-oriented mothers grew to twenty as they demonstrated in California's capital city, Sacramento. From there they went on to Washington D. C., where more than 100 mothers marched in front of the White House. They were determined to make a difference by reducing drunk-driving sufferers.

The efforts of that foundational group ultimately resulted in more than 360 chapters (still counting) throughout the world. A national commission against drunk driving has initiated more than 400 new laws in fifty states which address drunk driving.

Additionally, other organizations have caught the vision of making a difference. Groups such as (SADD) Students Against Drunk Driving and (PAAD) Performing Artist Against Drugs have joined the cause in their area of concern.

Our passions may be an indicator of God-given desires that must be directed by him. If you are one of those that needs to ignite your passion follow these simple guidelines.

1. **Make Christ your center.** When you make Christ the center of your life, all else has a way of falling in line. Trust the Lord with all your heart, acknowledge him in all your ways and he will direct your path. In other words, trust in the Lord and he will make sure you arrive safely at your God given destiny.

2. **Get mad.** Yes, I did say get mad. As Christians, we often think anger has no place. But it does. The Bible says, "Be angry and sin not." So, now that you know you can get mad, direct your anger at the right things. We can be angry at sin. With that anger and the energy, it brings, we can change things that may not ever change, otherwise.

We should be angry at injustice; we can work to change our justice system through the power of voting. We can help champion causes that need it. With our money, we can invest in the causes that matter to God and his divine purpose.

3. **Light the world.** Remember, YOU are the light. We are the light of the world. The Apostle Matthew quoting Jesus said it like this, "You are the salt of the earth...You are the light of the world. A city that is set on a hill cannot be hidden. Neither do men light a candle and put it under a bushel, but on a candlestick; and it gives light unto all that are in the house."

4. **Fuel your passion with your troubles**. Just like Candi Lightner did along with many others, we can fuel our passion with the troubles that come to us. Remember troubles come to us all.

5. **Stir up the gift that lies within you.** Stop waiting on something to happen to put you in action. Stir up the gift that's within you and act. Stir up the gift of speaking; stir up the gift of teaching and activate the call.

6. **Use the power of conviction.** Decide to use the power of conviction about the things that get us disturbed. Things that you can absolutely not stand by and watch happen. There's no one else doing anything about it; so you should.

7. **Develop excellence.** To develop excellence, aim high. Do your best in all things. Work as unto the Lord. Start habits of excellence.

8. **Set yourself up for success**. If you are just beginning, start small. Allow time for the passion curve. The more you fuel your fire, the brighter it will burn.

9. **Stir Enthusiasm.** Jump around. Get excited. Make some noise. The more excitement you express, the more contagious you become.

10. **Utilize the slow burn method.** Some things take time to manifest. You just have to wait it out. The one who waits for his/her time will be the victor.

Have you considered God may have lit your fire for a purpose? Or at the least allowed your fire to be lit. Luke, the physician instructs us, "No one lights a lamp and puts it in a place where it will be hidden." When we received Christ into our heart, we were lit for a purpose. I can only add God will place you where He wills.

Strengthening Your Step

The Light Of Fame

You are the salt of the earth...You are the light of the world. A city that is set on a hill cannot be hidden. Neither do men light a candle and put it under a bushel, but on a candlestick; and it gives light unto all that are in the house. —Matthew 5:13

Did you know our Father God calls us (the Body of Christ) and even gifts us with a measure of fame? One of the greatest powers of fame is influence. He has called us the children of light (Christians) to be an influence for good. In Scripture, Believers are described as salt and light. Salt preserves, flavors; light illuminates and brings clarity. Both are metaphors of God's call for us to impact and influence our society.

The Apostle Matthew quoting Jesus said it like this, "You are the salt of the earth...You are the light of the world. A city that is set on a hill cannot be hidden. Neither do men light a candle and put it under a bushel, but on a candlestick; and it gives light unto all that are in the house."

He goes on to say, let your light so shine before men that they may see your good works and glorify your Father which is in heaven. (Matthew 5:13a,14-16) Of course, we are all given a measure of fame. (light, influence) Each measure given is not the same. Just like in the story of the talents, each person was given a different amount. One was given ten, then another five and one was only given one.

As Christians, we are all famous in our area of influence. We are each given a measure of fame (influence) to grow and multiply. For some of us, we are famous in our family circle or our neighborhood. Others have been given regional or even worldwide fame and influence to spend wisely.

The truth is God has given us fame (the ability to influence) and along with this privilege comes a responsibility to use it for God's glory. From the moment we are in Christ (born again), we are especially empowered to influence others to good.

Are you using your influence to encourage someone? We can choose to use this power in a godly manner influencing others for the good. We all have an area of influence to be accountable for.

For example, are you influencing your spouse with encouragement, respect, admiration and your faith in God? Or are you influencing her/him with negative words, gossip and disrespect? What about your children? Are they being influenced by your gentle spirit or your temper tantrums?

There are some qualities to nurture to become the powerful Christian of influence God has created you to be:

1. The power of invitation. We as Christians have the power of invitation. We have the power to attract, lure, entice, urge, tempt, captivate and so on. Why because the power of Christ resides in us. Decide to use your power to invite others to obey God. Spend your invitations wisely. Make sure your invitations include inviting others specifically to Christ.

2. The power of good counsel. Are you the one everyone brings his or her problems to? Is it because you listen better than your comrades? I believe it's because God has gifted us with the ability to give good counsel through the Spirit of Christ.

Ask God for wisdom with any counsel you attempt to give. Sometimes, the best counsel is to listen and allow the Holy Spirit to whisper the answer to the person talking.

3. **The power of an encourager.** Are you influencing your spouse, your family, or those in your area of influence to God or away from God? Are the decisions in your life and family lining up with God's plans for your life? For example, God has called you and your family to a holy life.

Are you suggesting you go watch the latest R rated movie? Or are you influencing your family to obey God and purify your lifestyle?

4. **The power of enablement others.** Decide to use your power to influence to empower those around you. According to Webster to empower is to 'influence; to give power to or to enable.'

Every now and then we all need a little appreciation. Our families, our co-workers, our associates need to know they are affirmed and appreciated.

5. **The power of a good example.** Your life is often the only Bible some will read. Is anyone being influenced for Christ by the life you lead? Remember the wife of the unsaved husband.

The Apostle Peter's advice to her was even if her husband did not obey the Word of God, that he could perhaps be won over by her godly life and observing her purity and reverence (1 Pet. 3:1,2).

6. **The power of graciousness.** Have you learned the power of a soft answer, well-chosen words or silence? The writer of Colossians puts it this way, "Let your speech at all tines be gracious (pleasant and winsome), seasoned (as it were) with salt, (so that you may never be at a loss) to know how you ought to answer any one (who puts a question to you)" Col 4:6 AMP.

7. **The power of enthusiasm.** Stir to Action. Tap into your enthusiasm. Share your enthusiasm with others. It is contagious. According to the writer of Ephesians enthusiasm has the power to stir others to action. Rejoice in God's gifts to you and use them enthusiastically.

Then, beware of the top six enemies to good influence. I've listed some examples of women in Scripture that failed to use their gifts of influence for good. Each example points to a wrong choice to guard against:

1. **Used her power of invitation** to invite husband to sin. Eve, created to be a helper for Adam, invited him to join her in sin. (Gen. 2:18 and 3:6)

2. **Used her power of influence** to draw others away from God. Solomon's wives drew his heart away from God. (1 Ki 11:4)

3. **Used her power of enthusiasm.** She stirred others to evil action. Jezebel stirred up her husband Ahab to commit acts of abominable wickedness. (1 Kings 21:25)

4. **Used her power of counsel.** She gave evil counsel. Job's wife counseled him to "curse God and die." (Job 2:9)

5. **Used her power of persuasion.** She convinced or persuaded her husband of an evil plan. Rebekah willfully deceived her husband Isaac. (Genesis 27)

6. **Used her power of encouragement** to do the opposite. She despised her husband. Michal despised her husband David. (2 Samuel 6:16)

We as women in Christ are equipped with qualities for good influence. I exhort you to use your gifts to become influencers for Christ through the good you do. Let it be said that by the power of your influence you invited others to Christ, drew some toward God, stirred others to action, gave godly counsel and persuaded many to God's perfect plan.

Let your light of influence be a signal to the weary. Influence others to the good. Godly influencers empower, persuade, and convince others to the reality of Christ and to the common good.

Crossroads

Fueling Your Fire

I remind you to fan into flame the gift of God, which is in you. —2 Timothy 1:6b

Carman, a Christian recording artist, while visiting his sister as an east coast Italian kid, black Afro, silk shirt with black slacks, was radically saved (born-again) at an Andrae Crouch concert. His beginning in Christ is where songs like Serve the Lord and No Way Not Ashamed came from. He admits, "I know what it's like to serve. I served in my local church for about six years before going full time in the music ministry.

Those were hard years sometimes. However, I would not trade them because it taught me ministry. It taught me how to identify the Spirit of God. It taught me where and when the anointing was present. I learned when and when not to minister.

Through serving, I learned how to accomplish great things in the Kingdom of God. Any person who has ever done anything great for the Lord has dedicated years to the Lord. If you can handle the details, the mundane things of ministry, you can accomplish great things for God."

God's gifts and callings are without repentance, but the anointing may decrease and fade.6 I compare the anointing with the talents Jesus spoke of in His parable of the talents.7 The master gave one man a level one measure of anointing. Another received a level two anointing. Yet, another was given a level five anointing, each according to his ability.

Two of them used what he gave them and it multiplied. The one that received the level one anointing did not use his anointing and suffered great loss. Kenneth Hagin recommends going to the Lord if the fires of your anointing wane.

He remarks, "I went to the Lord about my anointing decreasing. He told me, 'If your anointing decreases, fast and pray until it comes back.' Now whenever the anointing fades, I wait upon the Lord in prayer and fasting and the same anointing comes upon me again."8 To keep your zeal and anointing burning hot:

1. Acknowledge your zeal and anointing may have decreased. I have learned the first step to any change is the acknowledgement that it needs changing. If you find yourself not doing the things you first did. Decide today to repent and go back to your first love (Christ). Our Father God awaits us with open arms.

2. Keep your first love first. We do well to remember the warning given to the Laodicea church, "I know your deeds that you are neither cold nor hot. I wish you were either one or the other! So, because you are lukewarm—neither hot nor cold—I am about to spit you out of my mouth." 9

3. Protect your anointing. We protect our anointing by living a holy separated, consecrated life. Our Father God requires that we be holy as He is holy.10 In my own life, God has gifted and anointed me to the discerning of spirits. He often enables me to see into the spiritual realm. The Holy Spirit has instructed me to guard my eyes (being careful what I allow them to see) as a part of the protection of the anointing in my life.

4. Become a student of the Bible. Study to show yourself a workman approved unto God and rightly dividing the truth. Many men of God started out great, but ended up religious fanatics because they became imbalanced somewhere along the way. All Bible and no Holy Spirit will often lead you off the path. On the other hand, all trying to be led by the Holy Spirit and no Word will leave you equally imbalanced.

5. Live a fasted lifestyle. Deny your flesh all it wants, often. The Apostle Paul admonished us in the race of life, "I make my body do what I want it to do so that after I have preached to others, I myself will not be disqualified." 11

6. Walk in love. How can we love God and not love our fellowman? Again, we gain instruction from the Apostle Paul simply paraphrased, "The gifts are useless in your life if you don't have love." 12

7. Live prayerfully. Jesus went apart often to pray and listen to the Father. We must follow His example to continue to walk in His anointing. Prayer prepares you for anointed service. Additionally, it helps you continue in anointed ministry. Get to know God in prayer and get to know His plans of service for you.13

Most people think of the anointing as something mystical that either you have or do not have. On the other hand, many mistakenly think God's power to do only rests upon those who publicly minister—preach, teach, prophesy, etc. I have heard it often said of someone, "He's not anointed to do anything. He has no ministry."

Yet, when I see this person operating in their gifts of administration and helps, I see the anointing. When I observe them doing the work of the ministry of helps, I recognize the anointing to serve. God's anointing empowers you to do whatever He calls you to do. If the Holy Spirit has gifted you to serve, begin to recognize and stir the anointing. Know that you have the anointing and equipment to do all that God created you to be and do. Now be sure to stir it up to the glory of God.

Spotlight

10 Passion Thieves Sent To Destroy Your Dreams

Make lemonade out of your troubles. What troubles do you have, waiting for you to use as fuel to your flame? Even, what mess can become your mission? Or what test will become your testimony?

With all that said, what has punctured your balloon? What let the air out of your sail? What rained on your parade? The Apostle Paul admonished the Corinthian church with similar language, "Who cut in on you? You were doing well.

So, now that we know there are enemies to our destiny, what shall we do? Glad you asked, here are ten things you can do to guard your dreams and the passion that fuels your destiny.

1. **Protect your dreams.** Be selective with who you share them with. But do share them.

2. **Stay focused.** Don't allow the good to destroy the best. When we allow ourselves to get too scattered in our focus, we stand a chance of losing out on receiving the best.

3. **Ignite others.** Share your enthusiasm. Don't stifle your passion. Take a chance. Be excited, show it and share it.

4. **Avoid critical people.** Know that criticism is contagious. It will spread to you and you spread it to others. Every now and then, I find myself in this mindset. I repent and ask the Holy Spirit to show me where I've gone wrong. It usually strings back to a hurt that I did not acknowledge and forgive.

5. **Put worry and anxiety under your feet.** These sins will choke the word of God and render ineffective.

6. **Keep good company.** It's a life's principle. Bad company corrupts good character.

7. **Watch out for discouragement.** Don't yield to discouragement. I know it happens to us all. Who can escape it? But make it a point to not stay long.

8. **Look for disorganization.** Stay organized. Don't let disorder run rampant in your life. Periodically take a day to organize and get things back on track. Order and cleanliness invites God into your circumstances in a profound way.

9. **Guard against half-heartedness.** The prophet said, "Here, take these arrows and shoot them out of the window." The king took the arrows and pulled the bow only a couple of times. The prophet of God was angry saying, "You could have totally destroyed your enemies if you had drawn the bow until all arrows were gone. Now that you have half-heartedly drawn the bow, you will only partially destroy your enemies."

10. Safeguard against comparing your dream. Don't compare your dream's progress with someone else's progress. Even comparing dreams can be risky. Too many times, we fall short in our own eyes with what we perceive someone else's progress to be.

Keep dreaming. But stay on guard against the dream and passion thieves. Things that are sent from the pit of hell to steal, kill and destroy your dreams and deflate your passion. Don't discount these things as insignificant. You and your dreams are designed to change the world. Count your dreams worthy.

Summary

Are you lit for a purpose? Candi Lightner, a normal housewife with children got mad after her twelve-year-old daughter, Cari was killed by a drunk driver. She found herself in the midst of her destiny, which caused her to almost single-handedly change a nation's complacent thinking about drinking while driving? Armed with a passion to help other mothers face similar tragedies, she formed MADD (Mothers Against Drunk Driving) and in the process turned her troubles into triumphs.

I was grateful to be reminded to make lemonade out of my troubles. It made me ask myself the question I asked you in the chapter. What troubles do you have, waiting for you to use as fuel to your flame? Even, what mess can become your mission? Or what test will become your testimony?

The efforts of that foundational group of MADD ultimately resulted in more than 360 chapters (still counting) throughout the world. A national commission against drunk driving has initiated more than 400 new laws in fifty states which address drunk driving. Additionally, other organizations have caught the vision of making a difference. Groups such as (SADD) Students Against Drunk Driving and (PAAD) Performing Artists Against Drugs have joined the cause in their area of concern.

When Jesus walked this earth he had a passion for helping God's people and destroying the works of Satan. Indeed, Scripture says, "For this purpose was the Son of God made manifest." His passion led him to his purpose and destiny (1 John 3:8). Discover your passion it may lead you to your purpose!

Destiny Challenge

Symbolic Illustration: Light a large candle and put it under a chair for a time. Then later, put it on top of a desk, table—wherever it can be seen. Explain the concept of this chapter: Turning Your Troubles To Triumph.

Chapter Five

Receiving Your Appointment From God

A Woman's Wild And Precocious Purpose Leads To Power

No one can receive anything unless God gives it from heaven. —John 3:27

She was born when it was not considered proper for a young woman to become a nurse. Her parents forbade it, society frowned upon it, and the medical professionals ignored it. Yet, Florence Nightingale changed the way the world viewed nursing and women. Where did she begin? She received her appointment from God.

Florence was said to be a precocious, intelligent child intellectually. Her father took particular interest in her education, unlike other young girls her age and status, he guided her through history, philosophy, and literature. She excelled in mathematics and languages and was able to read and write French, German, Italian, Greek, and Latin at an early age.

Never satisfied with the traditional female skills of home management, she preferred to read the great philosophers and to engage in serious political and social conversations with her father.

As part of a liberal Unitarian (Christian theology) family, Florence found great comfort in her religious beliefs. At the age of sixteen, she experienced one of several, what she described as "calls from God." She viewed her particular calling as reducing human suffering.

Nursing seemed the suitable route to serve both God and humankind. However, despite having cared for sick relatives and tenants on the family estates, her attempts to seek nurse's training were blocked by her family as an inappropriate activity for a woman of her stature.

Florence Nightingale changed the way the world viewed nursing. Her family traditions and the male dominated world at the time did not nourish her aspirations to serve the world.

Signpost to Destiny

A Wild Swan

Purpose or mission is determined by the development of values, balance, ethics, humor, morality, and sensitivities. It manifests itself in the way we look at life. —Luci Swindoll

Ms. Nightingale's call from God at a precocious age urged her in the right direction. Like most of us, Ms. Nightingale didn't receive an audible voice with lighting telling her what to do. But she did receive a call (a direction) from God at an early age. She, in essence received her appointment from God.

Going against the grain, she forged her commitment to God toward nursing. For nursing wasn't the profession it is today. She prepared herself and other women to be nurses. After treating and nursing only family members and close relatives to the chagrin of her immediate family. Her father agreed to let her quietly go study nursing in Germany.

In 1851, she entered the Deaconess School at Kaiser Werth in Germany for a short term of training as a nurse. The life there was hard and bleak, but Florence Nightingale gloried in it. She wrote her mother: "This is Life! I wish for no other earth, no other world but this."

She was an excellent student, and after her graduation, she returned to London and got a job running a hospital for gentlewomen. In 1853 she became the Superintendent of an Establishment for Gentlewomen During Illness, in London.

The fact that her patients were to be " gentlewomen" partly reconciled her family, but, even so, her mother did not understand her. With tears in her eyes, Mrs. Nightingale said, "We are ducks and have hatched a wild swan."

When You Receive your purpose and appointment from God

I've discovered when you receive your appointment from God everything changes. You'll want to do better and not only do better but act better. And if you act better and keep on acting better, you'll eventually BE better.

With that said, I have three principles I want to encourage you with after RECEIVING YOUR APPOINTMENT FROM GOD

When you receive your purpose from God – your perspective will change: You'll realize God is holding you accountable for what you do with his gifts. Remember Jesus' story of the talents in Matthew 25: 14-30. God gave me a paradigm shift years ago about my talent. I was sitting in a church service listening to a message about the man issuing talents and going on a journey. The man returns from his journey and discovers the one he issued 5 talents and the one he issued 2 talents doubled their talents. But the one he issued 1 hid his in the ground and did nothing. I heard this story countless times before and nothing happened.

This time was different; conviction from the Holy Spirit came on me and I began to weep. I clearly saw myself as the man with 1 talent who buried his gift. I knew I may as well have literally buried my talent in the ground just like the man for all the good I had done with it.

I prayed, "Father if you give me another chance, I'll develop it, I'll use it and multiply it." That 1 talent was my writing. I'm happy to report to you over twenty years later, with God's help I'm still doing my best to use it and multiply it. In fact, I'm certain my books would never have been born. For sure this article birthed from the books would never have been written if I hadn't prayed that prayer.

Speaking of doing your best, **when you receive your appointment from God you realize God deserves your best.** You'll serve in excellence according to Colossians 3:22-25

Bondservants, obey in all things your masters according to the flesh, not with eye service, as men-pleasers, but in sincerity of heart, fearing God and whatever you do, do it heartily, as to the Lord and not to men, knowing that from the Lord you will receive the reward of the inheritance for you serve the Lord Christ.

Don't just give God you any old kind of service. Make it your best. Let me mother you a bit, if you're serving in excellence you're going to be on time. If you can't be there – you're going to call and let your authority know what's up and reassure them you'll be back in place next time.

When Varn and I were taking a team of people to the highways and byways to feed the poor, we left at exactly that time. Our team members began to know if they truly wanted to go with us – they had to be on time. Make your service as unto God an excellent gift for His glory.

When you receive your purpose from God - you'll become more gracious. You'll realize you are an ambassador for Christ. Graciousness simply means to be kind, courteous, and compassionate. We should seek to serve our neighborhood, community, region, our world and each with the attitude of love. I know it sounds like a girly term. But it's not. Remember gentleness doesn't sound that manly either. But gentleness means strength under control.

When you walk in what God has appointed you to do in life, you'll seek to walk in forgiveness and gratefulness. If your sister in Christ offends you or one of your family members does something wrong to you - forgive. We're commanded to forgive.

I don't say that flippantly because I know the devil is a bad devil. And I know humanity continues to stoop to a new low but for God's grace. Many of you have horrible things to forgive. Yet, I say you can; with God, it's possible.

If not already, you will have opportunity to forgive. Someone will hurt your feelings. Some team member will treat you wrong. It's going to happen. How can I be so sure? Because, we're all just people right and people make mistakes.

Remember one of Jesus assistants' Peter coming to the Lord and asking how many times we should forgive (thinking he was generous) seven times. Jesus responded with, "No, Peter I say up to seventy times seven. Matt 18:21

Unforgiveness blocks our blessing. If we don't forgive it becomes sin in our life that may grow into a root of bitterness. It may even block your blessing of serving – your reward that God so longs to bestow on you.

When you walk in forgiveness with those around you, you are free to do what God has called you to do because you're grateful. Has God ever done anything for you?

My personal testimony is God found me a backslidden twenty-seven-year-old woman trapped in an abusive marriage and a sinful life style. He said through a friend, "I want you back."

To make a long story short, I recommitted my life to God. He set me free, cleaned me up, healed me and sent me a wonderful and caring husband named Varn and called us both into ministry. Has God done anything for you? Great! Then walk in forgiveness and let your service unto God—your life of purpose flow from a grateful heart.

Finally, serve with the purpose of God and expect His reward (Matthew 24) All over the world churches, businesses and corporations are looking for faithful people. They are looking for people who will sign-up for the long term. Divorce rate has risen to new heights. Now according to statistics you have less than a fifty percent chance that your marriage will make it. All over more and more, unfaithfulness is modeled as the norm.

People are known to have two and three careers as opposed to the twenty and forty year careers that used to be the norm. Why is it like that? I believe it's because sin abounds in our nation and our world. But through the gospel of Jesus there's hope. The writer of Roman says where sin abounds grace abounds. Furthermore, Father God has given us (the Christians) the ability and the command to BE FAITHFUL.

I want to be counted among the faithful, don't you? In that final day, I want to present my gifts and talents as multiplied. He promised a reward to those that serve Him faithfully. He says in Hebrews 4:10 he is not unrighteous to forget your work and labor of love which you have shown toward his name in that you have ministered to the Saints and do minister. I promise you when you take care of God's house, he will take care of yours.

I charge you to serve with an appointment from God. No matter what capacity you serve in whether it's nursing or some other field God has called you to work. I charge you to become gracious. I charge you woman of God --to walk in forgiveness, to be grateful.

I charge you to be faithful to the house of God and most of all be faithful to your relationship with God and he'll be faithful to you. And not only that but you'll receive the reward of faith God has in store for you.

PRAY WITH ME: Father God, I give my gifts and talents to you. I promise to use and develop my gifts even if it's only one. It's small in my eyes but you take it and make it big for your glory. Father, grant me a more gracious (kind) spirit. Help me to represent you. Father, forgive me for holding any grudges and I forgive anyone that has wronged me. I practice gratefulness for what you have already done in my life. Now, I fully expect for you to lead me and guide me into your purpose. Once, you show me I'll do my best to walk in it faithfully.

A Step toward Destiny

5 Signs To Finding Your Purpose

Commit your works to the LORD And your plans will be established. The LORD has made everything for its own purpose. —Proverbs 16:3,4a

Florence Nightingale kept preparing, practicing and training. During the Crimea War, it looked like her opportunity had come, they (Sidney Herbert, Secretary of War, and the War Office of England) called for her and the group of trained nurses, she had formed.

During the Crimean (cry ME un) War, she was put in charge of nursing. She went to the battlefield with thirty-eight nurses. At Marseilles, Florence Nightingale put in for a large stock of supplies. She did this in spite of the fact that she had been assured at the War Office that nothing was needed for the comfort of the wounded soldiers.

When she arrived, it was recorded she said, "The British high command has succeeded in creating the nearest thing to hell on earth." The hospital was a huge, dirty barracks* building. She got men to clean it up and managed to get the supplies they needed. It was said, no more than six shirts in a month had been washed before she and her teams' arrival.

Ordinary comforts for the sick and wounded were lacking and necessary surgical and medical supplies were often not forthcoming. To say the least, there were not enough beds, "there were no vessels for water, or utensils of any kind; no soap, no towels or cloths; no hospital clothes; no chairs, tables, benches, nor any other lamp or candlestick but a bottle."

Often the wounded men were left lying in the uniforms they had worn on the battlefield. It was evident that there had been a complete breakdown of medical arrangements at the seat of war.

Yet, Florence didn't give up. She kept pressing and with courage she applied herself and the team of nurses with her to the grueling task before them. It was often said, this assignment alone was the beginning of the proof of her calling. Her resolve, administration gifts, attention to detail, strict discipline for cleanliness and keen ability to bring order to chaos were as much needed as her skill and knowledge for nursing and statistics.

With all that I just described, Florence also organized a laundry house compiled of the wives who followed their husbands to the front lines. They collected and washed for the entire hospital.

She organized the kitchen where it began to produce regular and nutritious meals for the hospital staff and of course, the patients who could get well faster. Whereas, before they could only expect sporadic big boney and watery stews without vegetables.

It was in this chaotic but Kairos season, that Florence's calling and purpose began to be confirmed without doubt. It became evident that this is what she was born to do…

You may be like Florence and you received your call at an early age. Or you may be like others who received their call later in life. Whichever you may be, now is the time to get connected and fulfil your purpose in life.

Are you looking for your God given purpose? If nothing else, now is the time get started in the direction God's calling you. Here are five little signs to check for hints of your God given purpose along the way:

1. **Check your thought life.** What impressions are you getting? What thoughts keep popping up when you're quiet or prayerful? This advice, helped me a lot, in the beginning. My life was so busy with activity that I didn't have much time to look within.

But different seasons came, where I had the opportunity to be quiet and examine what I enjoyed thinking about. Until, those seasons came, I would search for a quiet moment. And I asked God to show me the time. I learned to grab those unredeemed times, we talked about earlier. I found times, like doctor appointments, car wash, kids practice, lunch hour, wee early and way late times when my family was asleep and more.

I would make notes. Those notes would turn into teachings that turned in classes that turned into books that turned into multiple series of books, courses and eventually events for women. So, just start.

2. Check for a divine dissatisfaction. Are you feeling dissatisfied about what you are doing? Or do you continually look for more. If so, it's a good place to be. Now, is an excellent time to make a change. There was a season in my life that I felt extremely dissatisfied with what I had accomplished. I kept feeling like there was more. And guess what, there was more. I kept searching; I kept knocking and eventually, the doors began to open. I started with the small. I started with where I was dissatisfied and kept pulling on the string...

3. Check what others are saying. I taught a WOW! Women of Worth class for a season, before I wrote the trilogy of WOW! Women books. My students kept saying, "Earma, you should write a book on this subject." I would respond. I think I will but it has to be when God releases me to do so. I want to write what he says.

Even with that said, I would store their words and encouragement in my heart, pondering the possibilities. Then one day, He Father God said, now it's time; go now and write it down for the generations to come.

4. Check your god given gifts. Examine your gifts and callings for your purpose. In the next section, we are going to examine the 'I Cames' of Jesus. He often expressed, for this purpose I came. It's the same for you and me. You know, for a certain purpose, we were sent to this earth.

On my journey to discovering my purpose, God has shown me he sent me as one of His writers. He showed me my calling as a prophetess, a teacher of the gospel and pastor. But, before it overwhelms, it didn't start that way.

When I first started talking to God about my purpose. He gave me a direction. He would only talk to me about my general mission as His woman, a godly woman, that's all in WOW! Women of Worth. You can get a copy at http://wowontheweb.com

5. Check your passions. What are you passionate about? What stirs you and lights your fire. Most of the time, you won't have to look far for the things you are passionate about.

But, I do realize, some of you may be right where I was, years ago. I was so beat down by life, that many of my passions had been snuffed out or so doused that I had to dig to find what even got me stirred up? Let me tell you, after I found it, there was no looking back.

I've been going full speed ahead. I can't say I haven't had any setbacks or water thrown on my fire. Because, I sure have had that. I've even had to dream again, a few times.

With God's grace, I keep going and building a bigger fire each time. I encourage you to keep going, keep dreaming, your destiny is shining brighter and brighter.

Pray and Ask God to show you what His purpose is for you. Notice the things that move you and make a list. And remember, Father God wants you to discover His purpose even more than you do.

Finally, think about it, your purpose is not just about you; it's what God delights to do through you. It's a lifelong partnership. Therefore, if you don't notice your thoughts leaning in a certain direction, a divine dissatisfaction, what others say to you about your purpose, your gifts and your passions, you are not only missing out on a wonderful journey yourself, but you are missing God's plan.

Because, He has called you to fulfil his purpose and wants you to walk in it — for others and for your own enjoyment and fulfillment.

Also, consider this. Since God has called you, He is completely able to reveal your purpose to you. You can know that He, most assuredly, will as you diligently seek Him.

He is no respecter of persons. He did it for Florence Nightingale; he did for me and he will do it for you. So, keep doing what's before you along with the things you know to do. It will all come clear, soon. (Hebrews 11:6).

Five Enemies to Purpose

The flesh (our human nature) is one of the greatest enemies to God's purpose in our life. The desire to do it our way, another way, the easy way, the short way or any old way besides God's way strives to dominate. Oh yes, there's the not-at-all pressure which is rooted in rebellion, one of the first mentioned enemies to purpose. Here are five enemies to guard against and protect your purpose:

• **Rebellion.** Because of the fall of humanity, we were all born into sin. So, we can safely say our nature is rebellious. That's why the Bible clearly says, the flesh is at enmity with God. Yet, Christ was born, lived a sinless life, died, was buried and resurrected. He redeemed us from the curse of the law. Through Christ, we died to sin and rebellion.

In Christ, we are the righteousness of God and live an obedient life. With all that said, rebellion will block God's blessings and His purpose. Rebellion will lead us off God's path and detour our destiny. We learned earlier, anytime we get off the path of God, we always stay longer and go farther than we ever thought we would.

• **Bitterness.** There are several top things that can turn into bitterness. Unresolved anger and hurt, unforgiveness, traumatic event, hardships are top culprits. Our enemy seeks to take advantage of these things in our lives.

We, all at one time or another go through things. And yes, the old saying is true, it's most important how you go through them. Many of us don't go through, we get stuck. If you suspect, you have a bitter root.

First of all, pray and ask the Holy Spirit to help. Give God permission to do what it takes to heal you. Then do the things He suggest one by one. A bitter root, you cannot pull it out yourself.

For me, it took courage to confess things, talking with a trusted someone and eventually I went through Christian counseling. If you are in the Dallas area, Jerry and Jessye Ruffin are a good source for Christian based counseling. Don't overthink it, just obey God's leading.

• **Unfruitfulness.** Bearing fruit is not hard. It's just what we do as healthy branches. God wants and is displeased when we do not bear fruit. So, it's key to stay healthy and connected to the Vine, which is Christ. Know that he chose us, we did not choose ourselves.

In him, we will bear fruit, healthy fruit that will remain. Prayer, staying in the word of God (reading, studying and meditating) and going to a good Word of God based church will keep us healthy and attached to the Vine, our Lord Jesus Christ.

• **Procrastination.** God's timing is perfect. In his time (season) he makes everything perfect. In my immaturity, I've yielded to impatience or running ahead more times than I care to admit. Father God has taught me about his timing more and more over the years.

In Jesus story about the ten women in the wedding party waiting for the bridegroom to come and get them to usher them into the wedding, five of the women procrastinated about their oil and readiness to go, when he got there.

In fact, to show how important this enemy is, the five procrastinators missed their opportunity to enter in their purpose and even were rebuked for their carelessness in waiting.

In a similar way, inside the kingdom of God, there are strategic God moments that he will prepare us for. We have to become ready, stay ready and not yield to procrastination.

• **Disorganization.** Seek to stay organized. Father God is a god of cleanliness, order and organization. Satan hides and thrives in filth, disorder and disorganization. He is the creator of lies, deceit, and disorganization. Open the door to either of these and it will invite all the other evil sins. Years ago, my sweet ministry friend and I would carpool to a ministry site.

Sometimes, she would ride with my husband and I. But other times, I would ride with her. When I rode with her, I would climb in and my feet would be lifted on top of boxes and trash on the floor of her car.

I wouldn't say anything. I would just climb in each time. After more than several months, the Holy Spirit said, if she would clean up her car, I would heal her mind.

I didn't know how to say what I heard by the Spirit of God. So, I just whispered a prayer for her. A few weeks after that, I rode with her again. I opened the door and her car was clear, cleaned up, front to back. I screamed in joy!

What happened? She excitedly told me, how she kept thinking she should clean up her car, so when she had guest…Anyway, she went to the doctor that same week. He told her, she was fine and she no longer needed all the medications she had been taking.

You know I went home and cleaned house, my car and everything else that was cluttered. I wanted to see what purpose might be blocked because of my disorganization. Won't you join me in guarding against the enemies to purpose like bitterness, rebellion, unfruitfulness, procrastination and disorganization. We seek to each discover our god given purpose and fulfill the will of God for our life.

Strengthening Your Step

7 Steps To Walking Out Your Purpose With God Through Service

For God is not unjust to forget your work and labor of love which you have shown toward his name in that you have ministered to the saints, and do minister. —Hebrews 6:10

By the time Florence Nightingale returned home she had become a national heroine and was decorated with numerous awards including one from Queen Victoria. After the war, she didn't really appreciate the fame, but continued to work for the improvement of hospital conditions, military and common hospitals. She wrote to influential people encouraging them to improve hygiene standards in all hospitals.

She, also, founded a training school for nurses at St Thomas's hospital, London. It was after her return from the Crimea that some of her most influential work happened. She was a pioneer in using statistical methods to quantify the effect of different practices.

Ironically, it was said, she found that some of her own methods of treating soldiers decreased recovery rates. But, this scientific approach to dealing with hospital treatment helped to improve standards and the quality of care. It became the foundation for much of the standards and practices we consider common in our hospitals, today.

Did you know God remembers and favors his obedient servants? He, too has a reward system. Yet, God's word is full of what I call qualifiers. Meaning when God says, "if you do this, I'll do this. He expects an action of faith in return.

Now, it's true God loves the whole world and He gave his Son who died, was buried and rose again for us all. He rains blessings on the righteous and the unrighteous, like sunshine, seed, time and harvest laws, rain to water our crops and more.

God is no respecter of persons but he does make a distinction between the obedient and disobedient. There are certain blessings, rewards, favor and honor that come only to his obedient servants, those walking in His purpose for them to the best of their ability and using what they have been given. There are certain blessings that the unsaved and the disobedient, the inactive Christian or slacking church may never experience.

Why? Because when you serve, your faith is activated in ways that it may never become activated in any other way. You become a member of the MORE society. Activating your faith and purpose positions you to receive more, give more and do more.

Think about this? What if it were really true when you serve God through his purpose, your appointment from God, it becomes the hinge that would swing wide God's door of blessings?

When you serve, you use the key for God's treasure. For years I've heard God's ministers call Jeremiah 33:3 His phone number. You know the Bible says in Jeremiah 33:3, "When you call, I'll hear and answer and show you great and mighty things you knowest not."

All you have to do is call him up. If you've never heard this before, you must give it a try. Go ahead use God's phone number and see what he shows. I've called up several times with this phone number. He showed me some pretty awesome things to come, good stuff I knew nothing about.

Recently, during some Bible study time the Holy Spirit showed me God's bank account number. And guess what, we each have an individual account. Anybody want to know what God's bank account number is? God's bank account number is Isaiah 33:6

He will be a sure foundation for my times, a rich store of salvation and wisdom and knowledge; the fear of the Lord is the key to this treasure. Now read it this way: He will be a sure foundation for every circumstance we face, a bank of salvation wisdom and knowledge; serving the Lord is the bank account number to this treasure. - Isaiah. 33:6 para.

1. When you serve things are added to you; you become a seeker of God.

You know the Scripture, "Seek ye first the Kingdom of God and all other things will be added to you." Did you notice the qualifier was seeking God first? Just like we discussed earlier, we seek the gift giver before the gift is a right priority.

2. When you serve you are positioned to receive the rewards of the faithful.

All the faithful women can get excited, because you're positioned for reward, multiplication and promotion. The Bible says God is faithful to the faithful.

3. When we serve we're following the example of Jesus.

Then we become an example to others. You know the ones that are following us as we follow Jesus. Matthew 10:40-42 He who receives Me, and he who receives Me receives Him who sent Me…He who receives a prophet in the name of a prophet shall receive a prophet's reward…

And whoever gives one of these little ones only a cup of cold water in the name of a disciple, assuredly, I say to you, he shall by no means lose his reward. So when was the last time you gave someone in God's kingdom a glass of water? Are you ready to receive a reward? I know I am. I've served a lot of glasses of water. Won't you join me in expecting God to do what He says He will do?

4. When we serve God promises to heal, protect and strengthen us.

Psalm 41:1-3 Blessed is he who considers the poor; The Lord will deliver him in time of trouble. The Lord will preserve him and keep him alive…You will not deliver him to the will of his enemies. The Lord will strengthen him on his bed of illness; You will sustain him on his sickbed.

I've stood on this Scripture plenty times for myself and my family. I've even used it as I pray for the faithful but Saints in need that I pray for our church's altar. God hears his Word being spoken in faith and believed; He responds to our faith.

Have you faced any trouble lately in these trying economic times? Remember Psalm 41:1-3, fellow servant of God. He is ready to hear and answer your prayer too.

5. When we serve we become the obedient.

When we obey, through Christ we're positioned for the blessings of obedience listed out in Deuteronomy 28. I put you on assignment to meditate on the promises of blessings if you serve and walk in obedience.

You are obedient to serve God in your local church and that makes you eligible for the blessings. Don't let them pass you by because you don't know or because you don't think you qualify. Through father of faith, Abraham (Old Testament) you qualify!

6. When we serve we become a follower of Jesus, those the Father will honor.

John 12:26 If anyone serves Me, let him follow Me and where I am there My servant will also. If anyone serves Me, My Father will honor. Also, read Luke 6:31. If not already, your honor is on the way. Father God loves to honor His faithful servants. Keep going; keep walking, your time, your due season will surely come.

7. When we serve we begin to know how to prosper.

We begin to walk out our destiny, God's chosen path. We are friends of God. He shares secrets with His friends. Did you know the Word of God contains secret revelations that only available to the faithful of God? In Psalm 25:12

Who is the man that fears (reverence, serve) the Lord? Him shall He teach in the way He chooses (destiny.) He himself shall dwell in prosperity. ..The question is the qualifier. If you can answer yes then you qualify to receive and walk in your true destiny.

Back when we were just starting out volunteering in our local church ministries, we were in a meeting and our elders at the time prophesied, "It's a good thing that you've been using good planks and worthy wood, straight nails and building the best house you know how. Because you didn't know it but the house you've been building all these years is YOUR house. Of course we shouted and praised God for that.

But now I turn and prophesy the same thing to you, woman of God. It's a good thing you've been using good materials and building the best house of service that you know how! Because you may not have known it but the spiritual house you've been building is YOUR house.

It's your house of ministry. It's your home for your family. It's your business, you've been sowing seeds of time and dedication. Now continue to do the work of God through serving wherever he's called you. Your due season of purpose fulfilled and a new power of God is on the way!

Crossroads

5 Ways To Keep Walking In Divine Destiny And Purpose

For this purpose, the Son of God was revealed: to destroy the works of the devil. —1 John 3:8

Are we there yet? Are you walking in the divine destiny of God? Let me prepare your heart and mind with something many of us don't consider. The divine destiny journey is a life long journey. Even those of us who think we have connected with our divine destiny in this season and are faithfully walking it out.

It still has a sense of 'we've only just begun; we're just scratching the surface' feel to it. I'm working by faith and hoping with reverential fear and trembling that I will hear the words, "Well done, my good and faithful servant." And I can say like the Apostle Paul, "I've completed my task

But here's one thing, you can be confident in: he that started the good work within you is faithful to complete that which he started. My hope is that I can encourage you in your faith to keep going on your walking in your purpose journey no matter where you are in your walk. Here are some things that will strengthen you to keep walking in purpose and destiny.

1. Walk in purpose while working it out. Therefore, my dear friends, as you have always obeyed--not only in my presence, but now much more in my absence--continue to work out your salvation with fear and trembling... — Philippians 2:12

2. Walk in purpose knowing He will keep you. He will also keep you firm to the end, so that you will be blameless on the day of our Lord Jesus Christ. —1 Corinthians 1:8

3. Walk in purpose keeping your faith. Cast not away therefore your confidence, which has great recompense of reward. — Hebrews 10:35

4. Walk in purpose with right focus. Therefore, holy brothers, partners in a heavenly calling, keep your focus on Jesus, the apostle and high priest of our confession. — Hebrews 3:1

5. Walk in purpose while he finishes. And I am certain that God, who began the good work within you, will continue his work until it is finally finished on the day when Christ Jesus returns. Phil. 1:6

So, don't get too caught up in what you can't do or haven't done at this moment. All that matters are you're on the journey that God has called you to participate in, whether it's as a great mother, a wonderful leader in business or administrating a ministerial gift.

Remember it's God that chose you to do what you are doing. Your job is to trust him and lean not to your own understanding.

What I mean is you may not always understand everything along the way. But you can be sure that your Father God is faithful to complete the good work began in you.

Spotlight

Who Cut In On You

Yet he has no root in himself, but endures only for a while. For when tribulation or persecution arises because of the word, immediately he stumbles. —Matthew 13:21

Have you seen a ship wreck lately? It's a painful sight to see. Usually the ship is all busted up. Its contents, crew members and passengers are strewn all over the place. Some are floating in the water nearby; suitcases, food, animals all float by. The ship has run aground or busted on the rocks. The point is the ship cannot go any further. It must be repaired or even reborn before it can sail again.

In a similar way, our faith is like a ship sailing on the seas of life. And like its natural counterparts, our faith ships can be wrecked by storms, troubles and even something or someone cutting in on our path to serving in God's Kingdom and ultimately fulfilling God's purpose and destiny in our life.

The Galatian writer said to the Galatian Church and now us, "You were running the race nobly. Who has (hindered and stopped you) from heeding and following the truth? (Galatians 5:7) Varn and I have seen and heard of many shipwrecks lately.

Even more are headed for a shipwreck, if they don't heed the Word of God. So, the Holy Spirit put on my heart to write to you about it. Hopefully, it will change someone's course after reading this little section.

To be honest, I came perilously close to shipwreck a number of years ago. I was so hurt and offended by some of my Christian brothers and especially sisters. By the grace of God, I avoided my faith's shipwreck by following close after the truth. I had to forgive, bless and keep on forgiving and blessing.

Remember the Story of the Sowers word in Matthew 13 and Mark 4 where it says in part, "...when trouble or persecution arises for the word's sake, immediately they stumble." In that season, I had to choose over and over again to accept the word of forgiveness and release my offenders, so I would not stumble or shipwreck in my faith.

If you are in the middle of persecutions or troubles that have risen out of seemingly nowhere, consider this it may be because of the Word of God active in your life. It may be quite literally, because you've discovered your purpose and you're on the journey. Meaning it may be because you decided to work wholeheartedly in your purpose as the woman of God, he has called you to become.

Or because you decided to come alongside your leader and help no matter who acknowledges what you're doing. Wait, one more scenario maybe you decided to walk in love regardless of those trying to offend you. Follow our Lord's instructions, accept the Word, obey it and bear the good fruit of love, forgiveness and longsuffering. Then, keep going to your destiny.

Summary

Have you received your appointment from God? Florence Nightingale was born when it was not considered proper for a young woman to become a nurse. Her parents forbade it, society frowned upon it, and the medical professionals ignored it.

Yet, Florence Nightingale prepared her life and those she influenced. She was literally ready for her Kairos season. Through courage, skill and readiness, she changed the way the world viewed nursing and women.

Where did she begin? I was encouraged and delighted to discover she received her appointment from God. (I hope you were too!) She received her appointment in the garden of her parent's wealthy home in Norkshire, New England.

She persevered through the persecution and antics sent by her family to defer her work in this field. It seemed the more determined they became, the more she forged forward to get training and stay prepared.

Prepared for what, you may have been asking. She didn't know her biggest challenges lay ahead. No one knew the Crimean War was in their future. But through preparation and training, she was able to rise to her Kairos season.

Yes! I am still reeling from the fact that no one knew what to do with the horrific conditions in the military hospital before she arrived with her team.

Getting your appointment from God is the best advice is the best you can ever receive. It's as simple as that. Ask him what your appointment is and he will show you. Remember Prophet Jeremiah instructed us with God's thoughts that are for our good, not for bad.

God thinks about the good and happy ending he has in store for us. Keep it moving. Stay on the journey. Prepare for your Kairos season. It may take some time. But it will surely come; for He is faithful to keep his promises.

Destiny Challenge

Symbolic Illustration: Create a sign with the concept or words that are the greatest sign to your purpose. Use a decorative wooden sign, poster board, manifesto or a page in your scrapbook.

Chapter Six

Praying through to Power

A Woman's Prevailing Prayer Power

The fervent prayer of a righteous woman has great power and produces wonderful results. —James 5:17b para.

*T*he call of God and her destiny was wrapped up into the development of this virtue. After years of trial sent to help her develop it, Kathryn Kulhman is considered the beloved woman of God extraordinaire because of her faith, perseverance and relationship with the Holy Spirit. How did she develop such prayer power with God and encouraged others to come on the journey? She persevered and found power with God.

Kathryn Kuhlman was born-again at the age of fourteen in the Methodist Church of Concordia, Missouri. In her own words, she said of that experience and her ministry: "It was the beginning of something that changed my whole life.

All that I knew was the glorious new birth experience, and (as a young girl) when I went to preach to those farmers in Idaho, I could tell them nothing more than what I had experienced: that Jesus would forgive their sins.

So, I preached salvation all across Idaho to every farmer, to everyone who would listen; but gradually I began to realize there was someone besides the Father and the Son - there was this Third Person of the Trinity. I felt compelled to know more regarding Him and, as I began searching and studying God's Word, I could see that divine healing also was in the atonement."

"It was in Franklin, Pennsylvania in the old Billy Sunday Tabernacle. I had gone to Franklin by faith (1946), not knowing what I would find there. It was in the third service, as I was preaching on the Holy Spirit, sharing with the people the little that I knew about that Third Person of the Trinity - a woman stood up and testified to her healing of a tumor.

That was the first healing that took place in this ministry. It happened without the laying on of hands, without any special prayer; it just happened as a woman sat in the audience while I was preaching on the power of the Holy Spirit. Since that time, there have been thousands and thousands of healings. *What is the secret?* It is the Third Person of the Trinity - the Holy Spirit!"

Kathryn Kuhlman always pointed men and women to Jesus, emphasizing that the greatest miracle was the transformation of a life. She often said:

"I believe in miracles with every atom of my being...because I believe in God - but Kathryn Kuhlman has nothing to do with the healing of sick bodies. I have no healing power. It's the power of God that does the healing.

The only part I have in it is making Jesus real to the hearts of men and women. Any results there might be in this life of mine, is not Kathryn Kuhlman. It's the Holy Spirit; it's what the Holy Spirit does through a yielded vessel."

In the biography of Ms. Kulhman, we discovered through it all, through failure, problems in her personal life and ministry, she persevered and found power with God. She went on to introduce the Holy Spirit to another generation in a way that had not been seen.

She prayed, persevered, and found power with God. Benny Hinn, noted tele-evangelist, and a host of healing ministry events attended by the thousands who openly, testifies that he believes he would not be where he is today, if it were not for Kathrn Kulhman and her meetings.

Signpost to Destiny

The Audacious Power Of Ask

Ask me and I will tell you remarkable secrets you do not know about your future and destiny. —Jeremiah 33:3 NL

May I be transparent with you? I used to consult my horoscope, tarot cards, psychics, spiritists, a lot, before I became a Christian. After I became a Christian, I found out it is highly offensive to Father God when we do these things. It's considered sin before God for us as Christians to conduct séances, read the cards, consult inner guides other than the Holy Spirit of God. So, you know how it goes, when you know better everyone expects us to do better.

It's the same way with God. When we don't know any better, we perish for lack of knowledge. Sometimes, we wonder why we can't overcome certain strongholds or get rid of addictions. It's because, the door is open through this sin. But when we know better, he expects us to do better. When I found out. I burned all of those books, pamphlets, whatever related material and rid my life of it, never to go that way again.

The last psychic, I went to see before Christ was Lord in my life, she told me a few things. I agreed they were all true, then I looked at her for more. But she had a strange look on her face. I asked her, what is it? I was highly curious by now. She said, "Are you Catholic. I keep seeing you walking and every few minutes you stop to pray for someone."

I returned, "No, I'm not Catholic. I haven't even talked to God in a very long time." "You must be Catholic; I keep seeing that. Are you sure?" Then she abruptly stopped the session and said, you can go now. She looked afraid. I left. In a few months, I had re-committed my life to God. The rest is history. I repented and renounced all connections with the devil and his kingdom.

But wait! Before you tune me out as too religious. I believe Father God put that desire in us to seek out our good future, even our destiny. This is what I have been preaching for quite some time now. God has a beautiful finish in store for each of us. His plan includes a bright future. He not only wants us to know it but he wants us to walk in it. Yet, we have to follow his word and do things his way.

With that said, here's a scripture the Holy Spirit taught me. I call it God's phone number. Ask me and I will tell you remarkable secrets you do not know about things to come. Jeremiah 33:3 These days, God is the only source, I'm asking about my future. He is the one and only true God.

Now, I do caution you to stay balanced. For we are growing a relationship with Father God. He's not a slot machine, quarter in and cash out. I noticed with the other stuff, it was really addicting with no relationship. So, I'm simply saying if you haven't prayed in a year or so, yet you want to use God's number. Maybe, you will or you won't hear from him. I do know you're his child and he loves you. So, why not ask Him about your future?

Years ago, I worked in corporate banking. The headquarters office, where I worked was a land of cubicles. Even in the land of cubicles there were better desk positions. For the last five years I worked for them, I always had a window cubicle with a very nice view. Several of my work associates came to me, and wanted to know how I managed to get such a desk.

There was a secret to the reason. It was so simple and in plain sight that they didn't believe me when I told them. So, they never acted on it. The truth was, I simply asked for it. The manager's position was in such high turnover, that in that five-year period, I rarely had to ask the same manager for my window desk.

So, each time our office moved, I would ask for my preferred seat. I'm sure God's favor and the fact that I was a hard-working team player played into it too. Even so, it never would have happened if I didn't take the courage to ask.

Proof of this, the five years before I started asking, my desk always landed in the row with everyone else, not in a quiet, secluded corner with an outdoors or garden view.

In a similar way, God's way in the kingdom of God, he has designed the audacious power of ask as an activator of faith. In fact, there are some blessings that come to us all automatically, like the sun loaded with vitamin D, rain that waters the earth, flowers that bloom seasonally, the law of gravity, seed, time and harvest laws. But there are other blessings that you only receive after asking.

Your life will play out regular, with nothing extraordinary, if you don't have the faith and courage to ask. Here are some things to be sure to ask for, if not already. After that, pray and confer with the Holy Spirit and ask for the promises of God designed for your life:

1. Ask to receive Jesus as Lord and Savior of your life. According to, Romans 10:9,10 that if you confess with your mouth Jesus as Lord, and believe in your heart that God raised Him from the dead, you will be saved; for with the heart a person believes, resulting in righteousness, and with the mouth he confesses, resulting in salvation. All Christians have received Jesus as Savior but many have not received him as Lord of their life. We must do both in faith.

2. Ask to be filled with the Holy Spirit. Simply pray, Father, please fill me with your Holy Spirit. I want to serve you on a new level, with new power and purpose. You are simply asking Father God to empower you by His Holy Spirit to do his will (your purpose.) Know you are asking according to God's word.

Read Matthew 7:8,9,10 "For everyone who asks receives, and he who seeks finds, and to him who knocks it will be opened. "Or what man is there among you who, when his son asks for a loaf, will give him a stone? "Or if he asks for a fish, he will not give him a snake, will he "If you then, being evil, know how to give good gifts to your children, how much more will your Father who is in heaven give what is good to those who ask Him!

And according to 24:49 Jesus says virtually the same thing. "And behold, I send the promise of my Father upon you; but stay in the city, until you are clothed with power from on high."

3. Ask God to show you your purpose. Of course, if you've been on the journey long with the WOW! Women books, you already know God's phone number. But just in case you don't know it, it's Jeremiah 33:3 NL Ask me and I will tell you remarkable secrets you do not know about your future and destiny.

4. Ask Father God to give you your destiny. By now, you know exactly what I'm talking about. Ask for your God ordained blueprint and plan for success, expected end and future hope. You know the same language God proclaimed to us through Jeremiah 29:11 when he said, "For I know what I have planned for you,' says the LORD. 'I have plans to prosper you, not to harm you. I have plans to give you a future filled with hope."

5. Ask Him for his recompense. Get to know Father God as Jehovah Gmolah, the Lord of Recompense. He has declared Vengeance is his and he always recompense. Repeat after me, "Lord write the story of God's recompense in my life, so that I might tell it."

Jesus explained it to us like this Satan's purpose and the reason he came but for to steal, kill and destroy in your life. But my purpose, the reason I came was so you might have life (our God ordained destiny) and that more abundantly."

We talked about this earlier. But some blessings are on the other side of choice. God has made sure, the power to choose is protected. He has placed the ability to ask as an activator of faith. So, there's only a few things left to do. We should get busy asking for His promises.

A Step toward Destiny

The Five Powers Of Ask

The weapons we fight with are not the weapons of the world. On the contrary, they have divine power to demolish strongholds. —2 Corinthians 10:4

Get your plans, your strategies from God. He'll take you by the hand and help you. There are times you won't have to fight for the battle is the Lord's. There are other times you must fight the good fight of faith, using weapons that not carnal but mighty to the pulling down of strongholds.

So, keep praying and ASKING to God to bless you, increase you and enlarge your territory. He will. It's his good pleasure to do so. Just be ready for the conquest, taking dominion and to occupy the good land (promises) he's given you. It takes pressure and sometimes pain to get you to the next level.

Don't be dismayed and confused about what you're going through. Ultimately, Jesus has given us the victory. The writer to the Corinthians said it like this, "Now thanks be to God who always leads us in triumph in Christ... (2 Corinthians 2:14) Trust God and know that He is in control. Listen to Him, follow Him, submit to the process and He'll get you there safely.

Have you ever had a prophecy or a word of knowledge spoken over you of something that is to happen in the future? Well, it's not going to come to pass in your life unless you start praying it out and asking God for it. It doesn't just come to pass automatically. Any failure in life is a prayer failure.

1. The Promise To Those Who ASK

For everyone who asks receives; the one who seeks finds; and to the one who knocks, the door will be opened. -Matthew 7:8

2. Asking With The Power of Agreement

...that if two of you shall agree on earth as touching anything that they shall ASK, it shall be done for them of my Father which is in heaven. -Matthew 18:19

3. Asking, Seeking, Knocking

ASK and it shall be given you; seek and ye shall find, knock and it shall be opened unto you: For everyone that asketh receiveth. - Matthew 7:7-8

4. Ask, Believe And Receive

And all things, whatsoever ye shall ASK in prayer, believing, ye shall receive.

5. Abiding In The Vine And Asking

If you abide in me, and my words abide in you, ye shall ASK what ye will, and it shall be done unto you.

What promises have the Holy Spirit shown you in the word of God? What prophetic words have you received? Yes, you know what to do, now ASK and receive.

Strengthening Your Step

Dare To Dream Again

Whatever your hand finds to do, do it with all your might. —Ecclesiastes 9:10a

I have six sisters and two brothers. Needless, to say we are a family of predominately girls. So, sometimes we are identified by birth rank or what number you are in the girls. For privacy, in November 1965 the last girl was born in our family.

We celebrate her as a beautiful person. Even so, her start was rocky at birth. Her legs from knees down to her feet were turned slightly inward, so she didn't walk for a long time. Her speech development was abnormally slow. The doctors kept saying in response to questions about when she would talk, "We'll see."

She was almost two before we knew she would talk. When she finally did, she had the sunniest personality. When she smiles on a rainy day, you think the sun came out. (cheesy but true) She wore leg braces a long time as a toddler. Now her legs are the straightest and best formed in the family.

I noticed something else growing up around my special sister. Good things would seem to come to her without effort. Like when we were teenagers, and we all went shopping for school clothes.

We, my other sisters and brother were serious bargain-hunting type shoppers. Well, the sisters were anyway; I couldn't say the same for my brother. My sister would walk around talking to people or doing everything but shopping.

When we got home, my other siblings and I would take out our clothing, looking over the great deals we got. Without fail, most of us would have something that didn't quite fit like we thought it would. To make a long story short, each piece of ours would fit my sister like a glove and like she picked it out herself. I mean the colors were perfect, too.

So, fast forward to adulthood. My sister progressed leaps and bounds in development as a child to adulthood. Through special education, she received her diploma. But she still wasn't able to legibly fill out any type of application, along with other needed skills. She needed life skills like counting and budgeting money, paying household bills.

So, it looked like she would have to live with our mother for the rest of her life. That would be, o.k., if one wanted to do so. For her, she's always wanted the independence of living on her own. It was her big dream to live on her own.

In fact, one day (me and each of my siblings had moved away from home) my mother called me and said, "Could you talk to her? She won't stop crying. She says she's going to run away…"

I found out a lady in the community had moved out of her mother's house. Although, the lady was much older, she also had lived at home with her mother for a long time. So, after she moved out; someone said mean things to my sister. Like, you'll never move out. You'll be at home the rest of your life…

So, I instructed my mother to go ask her if she would talk to me or just listen. When she came to the phone, I asked her if she would tell me what was wrong. Knowing my mother had already given me details of her wanting to run away. Yet, I wanted to hear what she would say.

I had compassion for her plight. I've always had the GO in my inner being. I recognized the same thing in her. I knew how miserable and frustrated I would feel, if I didn't have my independence.

I listened; not understanding most of what she was saying. But feeling her pain so deeply that I began to cry too. Then it burst out of me, "Give God A Chance! Give him a year and see what he does. Give him that time to work something out. I just feel something is going to happen for you. He knows how you feel…" Long story short, she said o.k. and we ended the call.

About a year to the week, my mother called and put my sister on the phone. She said, "I got a place!" Of course, I said, "What do you mean you got a place?!!!" Her reply was, "I'm moving in Thursday."

I burst into tears. All I could say was, "You remember last year when we talked…" The details don't sound near as glamourous; that is if you don't know the before and after of this miracle (to us).

My sissy is now living her dream in an assisted living apartment building, about fifteen miles from my mother. She attends a life skills center five days a week. And someone is assigned to her to oversee paying bills, washing clothes, grocery shopping and other life skills that she couldn't manage on her own.

I'm simply saying, my sister with special needs had a dream that she kept pursuing and asking; it eventually came true. The fulfillment of her dream, inspires me to keep asking, keep knocking and pursuing my dreams. As a result, I came up with five life lessons that I've learned if you need to Dream Again, and most importantly, if you need to give God a chance:

1. Flip Your Perspective. Varn and I delivered a message to a group of servant leaders and armorbearers called the 'Precious Gift Of Impartation.' Within that message, we talked about flipping your wrong perspective to a right perspective.

Let me tell you, if you've ever experienced hardship, persecution or troubling circumstances it's pretty easy to get a wrong perspective. For me back then, we were being persecuted for something we didn't even do in the first place…

Varn turned to me and encouraged me to do what we have been preaching all this time to others, "Flip it." It was time for us to flip our perspective and count precious all the things we had received. It's your time.

Not assuming everyone is going through troubling circumstances but if you are there right now, you have to go through and find the lesson (s) God is wanting you to learn and count them precious. When you can do that, you know that you've successfully flipped it.

2. Get A New View Of Failure. Thomas Edison famously gave us a new view of failure. It took him more than 10,000 attempts to invent the light bulb. He said, he didn't look at those 10,000 attempts as failures but as experiments because he learned from each one of them what not to do and what didn't work.

My point is somewhere along the way, he figured out what did work. The rest is history, his name resounds across the globe because of his tenacity and dream for a brighter future with people turning on a lamp with a light bulb to light their lives.

Know that all of life can become an experiment with this little tweak in your thinking. We all want a brighter, bigger, better future. All we have to do is pick ourselves up, get a new view of failure and learn from each mistake.

3. Do The Dream With All Your Might. The Biblical King David was a man of principle and passion. He is famous for doing whatever he did with all his might. Remember, he danced with all his might when they brought the Ark Of The Covenant to reside in the city. Recently, during a study of his life I noticed a little phrase I had never noticed before.

It says, "King David 'prepared with all his might' for the building of the temple. Take a minute, examine your life. Can you say you're doing your dream with all your might? Can you say you're doing anything with all your might?

If so, yeah, keep going! If not, here's the thing, you can change that, you can start now. Here's another voice of encouragement, the Ecclesiastes writer said, 'Whatever your hands find to do, do it with all your might."

4. Dream Again. At this point, I have another question. Have you ever had a major setback? Did things not work out like you thought? You lost the house anyway. You went to prison. The school you were putting your life's work into closed. You lost what was considered by everyone, including you, your perfect job. Have you even experienced a valley where you had multiple setbacks or challenges that led to failures?

The reason I mentioned more than several categories is because dreams usually die in either of those circumstances. Not long ago, I went through a valley in my life that caused a major setback.

While in the valley, I began to think about other points in my life that the same kind of epiphany (different details) came to me. I had to make the same kind of decisions to Dream Again. So, I encourage you whatever the circumstances may have been, Dream Again.

5. Give God A Chance. Even with all the encouragement, I've just given you there's one more perspective that I must mention. Just like I told my sister during her time, I must tell you, Give God A Chance. It really is true, God can work it out much better than we can. The battle really is not ours. The battle is the Lord's battle.

Promise to do only what he prompts you to do toward this dream. Then when he prompts, leads, do it with all your might, quickly. God's timing is very important. His timing is perfect. When I wrote my first book, a troubling circumstance rose up. It was so intense, I put the book down with intentions of never picking it up again.

So, much to my surprise I lost the anointing in my other projects. I went to Father God with my concern, He immediately said to me, "When you go back to what I first told you to write, there you'll find the anointing. I did and it was. I finished that first book He gave me and I'm still on the journey. So, give God a chance. He will not disappoint you.

What dream died in the valley of circumstances that surrounded you? Maybe they were even sent to snuff out your dream. Either way, it's time to Dream Again! Only this time, give God a chance. He is for you.

Remember, if God is for you who and even what can really stand against you. I'm dreaming again. I've released it and giving God a chance. Won't you join me? Let's dare to dream again and do awesome things together in Christ.

Crossroads

Waiting In The Wings Of Life

He has made everything beautiful in its time. He has also set eternity in the human heart; yet no one can fathom what God has done from beginning to end. —Ecclesiastes 3:11

Are you waiting for your season to change and the promises of God to come to pass? Don't worry; you're not alone. We all have to wait on the Lord for a season at one time or another. Our timing is usually not the same as God's. So, what do you do in the process? You know while you're waiting, what do you do?

This can especially be difficult for women who are movers and doers in the Kingdom. All the type A personalities, mothers and business professionals feel like they have to do something all the time. I believe Martha (Jesus' friend) was in that category. Here are some things, over the years I've learned to do more and more while waiting:

1. Thank the Lord. Cultivate gratefulness; for you know He's faithful to do what He's promised. Thankfulness will keep your heart open and ready to receive when your promise finally does arrive. Whether you are waiting for the wife or husband of your dreams to appear in your life or a sack of groceries for dinner this week, God will fulfill.

2. Look for the learning opportunities. Years ago, my niece was baby-sitting our 5-year-old at the time. She told him to come and sit down. He said no; I don't want to sit down. Her response was, "We can do this the easy way or the hard way. Either way, you're going to obey." Aren't we just like that with God?

Usually our waiting season is filled with teachable moments. We can wait the easy way, trusting and learning. Or we can do it the hard way, kicking and mumbling against the season the whole time. I'm learning more and more to embrace the season and look for my learning opportunities.

3. Grow in self-control. While we are waiting, we have to exercise patience. The more we exercise patience, we grow in self-control. I've discovered our disobedience and rebellion are sometimes birthed out of impatience. Impatience with what, you might ask. When the wait is long; we get impatient with the plan of God.

When we have to wait, it puts the squeeze on our character. What comes out depends on our maturity and how much we've grown in self-control. So, during your season get control of yourself, exercise some patience and wait. Your promise is on the way.

4. Don't give up. This one is easier said than done. At least for me it has been. Early in my Christian walk, I was respectfully complaining to the Lord, "Most people I pray for get their prayers answered and I rarely see any of mine answered." I prayed, believed and waited for God to answer. I thought he was going to say something like, "Whine, whine is all I hear out of you. At least you woke up this morning..."

But He didn't; he responded graciously to me with a mini vision. "I was sitting high up and looked down and saw myself praying from a list. Yes, it was a long list. But my answer was in the one thing that stood out in the vision. I would pray with focus and fervency for one thing on my list.

From where I was sitting in the vision, I could see whatever I was praying for coming with speed. One thing I was praying for back then was a car. My car had stopped working and I needed transportation. I saw the car coming toward me fast as I prayed.

Then I would stop praying; lose focus and move on to the next thing. I saw myself do this three different times. Each time I saw whatever I was praying for would be (at the door, within my grasp, right around the corner) but as soon as I stopped and lost focus it would turn around and leave faster than I saw it coming. Then I woke up.

I immediately knew the simple truth the Lord was communicating to me. Perhaps you recognized it too. I gave up too soon. Like the car I was praying for: I saw the car coming toward me as I prayed. It was almost there but I lost patience and gave up believing.

So, my point is: I learned to focus on 1-3 things in prayer and don't give up until I see it. I'm not saying I have received everything I've asked for over the years since then. But I can say every prayer has been answered. And so will yours if you pray in faith according to God's word and wait in faith and patience until it comes.

Spotlight

The Divine Yes

For every one of God's promises are "Yes" in him; therefore, also through him the "Amen" is spoken, to the glory we give to God. —2 Corinthians 1:20

Years ago, my then pastor asked me to stand up in a church service to receive a word of prophecy. His words were, "God says he's going to settle you. No more will you be tossed about. No more will you move with uncertainty. I'm settling you starting from the inside out. Like Me, your yes will be yes and your no will be no..."

The Divine Yes

I can testify God has done this in my life. I've become a finisher. My yes is a yes. I follow through. My family, my friends, my world and now my ministry are beneficiaries of the stability that God has worked in my life.

More importantly, I've learned this about our God. We can depend on Him for the divine yes. Through His word, he has given us a divine yes in all things concerning life, death and throughout eternity. If it's salvation from trouble, you have a yes. Maybe, it's healing in your body, through Christ Jesus, God said yes!

Many live in poverty; because they don't know God said yes to prosperity that overrides the curse of poverty in their life. Or perhaps, you're like I was, unstable with lots of maybes and yeses that turned out to be nos. God intervened in my life with His divine yes. He settled me and made me firm in Christ.

I used to bring up all the reasons, I was so unstable. Like all the bad things that happened to me that made me this way. One day, I dropped all the excuses; I mean reasons; I took responsibility for my sins, my short comings and said, "God help me. I confess, I've been like water and the wind, turning whichever way my circumstances turned me. I've been unable to change myself, help me..." Then came the word of prophecy. The rest is history.

God's Confirmation

Not long after that, I was reading scripture and the Holy Spirit confirmed what Father God had done for me through the words of the Corinthian writer, "No matter how many promises God has made, they are "Yes" in Christ. And so through him the "Amen" is spoken by us to the glory of God. Now it is God who makes both us and you stand firm in Christ. He anointed us, set his seal of ownership on us, and put his Spirit in our hearts as a deposit, guaranteeing what is to come."

Show Up And Stand Up

You know if you recognize that instability in yourself, He wants to do the same for you. For some of you, it plays out like this. You agree to help in your local church but you consistently don't show up. Or you show up but you're not serious or committed in what you do.

If it's a sign of a deeper instability, ask your Father God for help. If it's within your decision and will to do better, do it. Change your bad habit. Show up and stand up with commitment and faithfulness. You can do it; choose today and our Father God will help you.

Yes To His Will And Way

Since, He has so graciously given us His yes, we need to learn to say yes to his will and his way. I firmly believe we become ready to receive the divine yes, when we can say yes to His will and His way in our life.

We become ready to live the blessed life. You know all the blessings of obedience the Deuteronomy writer describes flow through the divine yes given through Christ. We, literally, become vessels of honor and ready for the Master's use. Say yes to God's will and way and receive His Divine Yes!

Summary

Have you been clothed with power from above? The call of God and her destiny was wrapped up into the development of this virtue. After years of trial sent to help her develop it, Kathryn Kulhman became considered the beloved woman of God extraordinaire because of her faith, perseverance and relationship with the Holy Spirit.

In the biography of Ms. Kulhman, we discovered through it all, through failure, problems in her personal life and ministry, she persevered and found power with God. She went on to introduce the Holy Spirit to another generation in a way that had not been seen.

I was joyful to see the audacious power to ASK and the DIVINE YES emerge as one of the prominent revelations of this chapter. There came a fresh faith to ASK Father God for His promises. I remembered whatever we ask for according to his word, he hears us and if he hears we have what we've asked for.

Even while writing this book, I've suffered setbacks, disappointments and generally God's process in which I'm grateful for. I remembered Jesus explanation of Satan's true purpose to steal, kill and destroy along with his purpose embodied in his words, 'I came that you might have life more abundantly."

With that in mind, I was encouraged to dream again as I encouraged you to dream again. Finally, know that we serve a God of recompense, who is ready to give you your story of recompense.

Destiny Challenge

Symbolic Illustration: Sign up for the WOW! Women's 21 Days To Destiny Challenge.

Chapter Seven

Fulfilling Your Passion, Purpose And Power In God

A Woman's Power Propels Her Destiny

Strength and dignity are her clothing, and she smiles at the future. —Proverbs 31:25

W ho can find a woman of passion, purpose and power in God? Even in a selfie generation, her inner beauty surpasses her physical beauty. She is more precious than rubies. Her family can trust her, and she will greatly improve their life. She brings them good, not harm, all the days of her life. She walks in her destiny—her purpose from God and helps others to walk in theirs.

She finds commerce suited to her and busily works at it. She is like a merchant's ship, bringing her food from afar. She gets up before dawn to prepare *spiritual* food for her household and plan the day's work for her employees.

She goes to inspect a company and buys it; with her earnings she raises another company, providing for many. She is energetic and strong, a hard worker. She makes sure her businesses are profitable; her light stays on late into the night.

Her hands are busy fulfilling her purpose and destiny. She extends a helping hand to the poor and opens her arms to the needy. She has no fear of a winter season for her household, for everyone has provided for and with warm clothes.

She makes her own products. She dresses well and in style, fine linen and purple gowns, fit for every occasion. Her family is well known in the neighborhood and city, where they sit with the other civic leaders. She makes belted linen garments and sashes to sell to the wholesalers. (Fine linen stands for the righteous acts of God's holy people.)

She is clothed with strength and dignity, and she laughs without fear of the future. She looks forward to her destiny and fulfilling her purpose. When she speaks, her words are wise, and she gives instructions with kindness. She carefully watches everything in her household and suffers nothing from laziness.

Her children stand and bless her. If married, her husband praises her: "There are many virtuous and capable women in the world, but you surpass them all!"

Charm is deceptive, and beauty does not last; but a woman who fears the lord will be greatly praised. Reward her for all she has done. Let her deeds publicly declare her praise.

Signpost To Destiny

12 Powers That Propel Your Destiny

For what the law could not do, in that it was weak through the flesh, God sending his own Son in the likeness of sinful flesh, and for sin, condemned sin in the flesh: That the righteousness of the law might be fulfilled in us, who walk not after the flesh, but after the Spirit. —Romans 8:3,4,

The proverbial woman knows her purpose. So, after you know your purpose, you can begin to drive toward your destiny with assurance and confidence. You know that God has everything in control of your life, not your mother or father. Not even your spouse or your children or lack of children.

You know God's blessing is upon you. You know that you are destined to walk in God's purpose. You've asked. You're moving forward on the journey to your pre-destined place. Now, the question becomes, how can I be more effective in fulfilling my destiny? I have listed twelve energies that will continue to move us forward in fulfilling our destiny, successfully:

1. The power of urgency. Get a sense of urgency about fulfilling your passion, purpose and power in God. Know that we are as a shuttle flying through the night. Number your days aright. The writer of John said, "The day is almost ended, we must quickly fulfill our God given task for night is coming when no man can work." John 12:13

2. The power of love. We are as loud clanging cymbal, if we do not love. Love with the love of Christ, the Agape love. As you fulfil your destiny, in love, you grow fruit that remains. Fruit that our Lord Jesus can be proud of and announce to the world.

3. The power of forgiveness. A life full of the passion, purpose and power of God is a life unhindered, walking in forgiveness. Whatever you forgive, Father God forgives and whatever you retain, he retains.

4. The power of vision. Ask Father God for vision. As he gives us his vision, we are successful and walk in step with the Holy Spirit. I know many of us can easily write a vision statement for whatever we need to. So, what I'm encouraging you to do is get your purpose, strategy and a vision from Father God.

5. The power of clarity. Periodically, I pray that God will give me right focus. I lead a busy lifestyle as I suspect you do. But I don't want to get so busy and veer off what God wants for my life. To stay connected to the Vine, I do my best to keep right priorities and right focus, putting God first.

6. The power of excellence. Excellence is a habit that I practice and encourage you to do the same. Sometimes, we forget excellence and perfection are two different things. In fallen nature and humanity, there is no perfection to strive for. But we can seek to be excellent in all we do.

7. The power of diligence and hard work. A lot of people, these days, don't know what hard work is. I got my work ethics from growing up on a farm that was our family's business and livelihood. In other words, I grew up working hard. It carried over into our business and ministry. Even if you didn't grow up on a farm, there's lots of ways to apply and teach our children diligence. For one thing, do your best to become a finisher.

8. The power of compassion. Because of hurts and the pain of life, not many of us naturally walk in the compassion of God. With that in mind, pray and ask for the compassion of God to flow through you. Especially, if you've been called to God's ministry. Ask for his compassion for his people and see what happens. You might be surprised.

For example, the compassion of God flowing through me is what started this whole ministry, books, classes, everything. Years ago, I prayed before teaching a class to a group of rowdy maximum security women inmates. I asked for his compassion and what to say to these women. He said, "Tell them they're WOW! Women of Worth...

9. The power of enterprise. Use the power of enterprise in your life. I'm not only speaking of running a major corporation. Although, I know many of you are more than capable and do so, every day. Enterprise, simply means a large difficult undertaking. Which is why, I said earlier that women are built for such things whether it's in the home, in the public service sector or the corporate world. Speaking of enterprise, I really enjoyed learning and teaching about Florence Nightingale.

She was a perfect example of taking up a large difficult undertaking. You might remember, she was put in charge of the military hospital during the Crimean War. Although, it didn't quite mean what it would have meant today. Through her skills along with fortitude and skill, she changed the way the world viewed nursing and setup a foundation for modern day nursing.

10. The power of routine. Keeping a routine is similar to diligence. Set a routine and form habits. Habits set boundaries and safeguards in your life that you may not get in any other way.

11. The power of perseverance. Therefore, since we are surrounded by such a great cloud of witnesses, let us throw off everything that hinders and the sin that so easily entangles, and let us run with perseverance the race marked out for us (Heb. 12:1).

12. The power of passing the torch. Mentorship is a vital part of fulfilling your destiny and accomplishing God's will of keeping it going.

Stay connected. Again, we say abide in the vine. As with any power surge there is the potential to knock everything out and destroy some valuable items. But with the power surge connector invention, it controls the powerful currents so that the currents may safely supply power and energy to our electrical appliances.

A Step toward Destiny

Raising Your Expectancy For (A Happy Ending)

Strength and dignity are her clothing, and she smiles at her destiny. — Proverbs 31:25

There was a wealthy man that hired three women. He gave out talents, each woman according to her current ability. One woman he gave ten talents. Another woman he gave five talents. The third woman he gave one talent. Then he took a trip.

After a while, he came back to check on his investments. The word investment itself says, the wealthy man was expecting a return, right. The first woman with joy reported to her employer, look I have multiplied what you gave me tenfold.

The employer said, "Well done, my good and faithful employee! I'm increasing you to ten cities. The second woman also with joy, gave a good report. She had also doubled what was given to her. She showed her employer she had multiplied what was given to her to ten talents. The wealthy man gave his approval and rewarded her with an increase as well.

Finally, the last woman filled with self-condemnation, she lashed out at her employer saying, because I knew you were a shrewd man, gathering where you have not sown. I took my one talent and buried it. I thought to myself, "At least, I'll be able to give back to him what he gave me."

The wealthy man was upset with the woman he had given one talent saying, "Why didn't you at least put my investment in you in a bank. At least, it would have built up interest." Instead of approval and reward, he said, "Take what she has and give it to the one who had the most. Then throw this woman out." I've heard this story told most of my life.

But one day while sitting in church listening to it being told again, something changed in my heart. I felt convicted about my one talent. I repented and told the Lord I was sorry for burying my talent. I asked for another chance. I repeated the words of the minister, "Father take my small and make it big."

I've been busy multiplying what God gave me to start with. My one talent was writing. Father God has been multiplying me from faith to faith and glory to glory. Fifteen books later, I'm thankful. I didn't start as a publisher with a book ministry. I started taking classes and volunteering writing newsletters to my family, church departments and eventually business associates.

With that said, has your faith gone to another level, recently? Has your fame increased? Yes, I did say fame. Remember the story I just reminded you of was told to explain how the kingdom of God operates. In the kingdom of God, He expects us to increase in the things of God. You see in our generation and in the New Covenant of grace, we have been given much. And to whom much is given, much is required.

The great and precious gifts of faith love and mercy run rampant today through Christ. Centuries ago, civilizations could only glimpse the inventions, wisdom, knowledge and revelation from God that we experience today. Humanity suffered through the Dark Age, now we live through the Information Age, Digital Age and Technology, simultaneously.

In my mind, it's for the spread of the Gospel. So we can accomplish the Great Commission make disciples of the nations and so that every soul may have the opportunity to choose Christ.

So, to continue increasing in every area of life, here are six questions to ask yourself, periodically. It will keep you moving forward in Christ increasing in faith to faith and glory to glory. The first three are decisions and the last three are actions to confirm your decisions.

1.   Do I need to change my perspective?

2.   Do I expect to know and walk in my purpose and destiny?

3.   Do I believe that God has a plan and wants greater for me?

4.   Do I seek the kingdom of God first?

5.   Have I asked God for my appointment?

6.   Do I renew my mind with the Word of God?

Changing my perspective. Most of us need a perspective change at one time or another. Jesus is the lifter of our heads. He lifted my head when I was walking around with my head hanging down. Inside, I was humped over with my hands hanging to the ground like a monkey. But God gave me a new perspective—His perspective.

Along with that new perspective, I needed an inner healing. God gave them both to me. Maybe that's not your story. You may just have wrong thinking about whether God even wants to give you increase. Let me be clear, Father God wants His children to walk in their destiny. In fact, He promised to give us and our children more life.

Raising my expectancy. Now that you know it's God's will for you to walk in your destiny, raise your expectancy level. As a child with a parent, we can expect God's goodness and love. The word of God says, "So I say to you: Ask and it will be given to you; seek and you will find; knock and the door will be opened to you.

For everyone who asks receives; the one who seeks finds; and to the one who knocks, the door will be opened. "Which of you fathers, if your son asks for a fish, will give him a snake instead? Or if he asks for an egg, will give him a scorpion? If you then, though you are evil, know how to give good gifts to your children, how much more will your Father in heaven give the Holy Spirit to those who ask him!"

Deciding to believe. Then there's others of us, who just don't believe. When I find this in my mind and heart, I repent of unbelief and ask for God's help. We don't think Jesus meant what he said in the red letters of our Bible. One specific scripture is, "Greater works than these shall you do."

We have a tendency to think, Jesus is so great that he couldn't have meant that. But yes, he did mean it. He designed you and me for greater works, because we were born in this generation. And the next generation, we will be looking for more and even greater works.

Seeking first the kingdom. Normally, we don't think of Matthew 10:20 as a destiny scripture. But notice the last part of that passage is, "…all other things will be added to you." Jesus said, "Seek the kingdom of God and all other things will be added unto you." That includes your destiny. Follow God's ways and your destiny, your purpose will be added to you.

Getting my appointment from God. When we can say as the Apostle John said, we can only do what is given to us from heaven, we can ask God for our appointment. Say with me, "Father, what do you want me to do with my life?" I know this can be a scary question, especially if you've heard the stories about God's call to missionaries in distant lands, not seeing family for years. God is a faithful and just God.

Meaning, I can't promise you it won't be hard but I can promise you that He will be with you every step of the way. It's not about what we can or can't do. Although he equips us, it's more about our willingness. Our ability to take courage, let go and let God-be-God through us. Now, go receive your appointment from God.

Renewing my mind in the Word of God. It's God way, we have to renew our minds and life in the word of God. Not just on Sundays is not enough. We must read, pray and do the word of God daily. Many of you have heard this story. But it's worth repeating. I dreamed that I was watching a storm on the horizon.

It was a huge ominous black natured storm headed straight for me. I began to do all the things I heard you should do before and in a storm. I heard you should praise God. I repeatedly said, Thank you Jesus! Thank you Jesus! About twenty times. I heard you should hunker down, meditate and trust God. I had moments of silence to no avail...

The dream continued. The storm arrived and I was being destroyed like the wicked witch of the west. I woke up and said aloud, "That's not scriptural!" The Holy Spirit responded, "Oh, but it will be if you don't do what I've been leading you to do. Read the Word of God."

That day I went and got a daily reading Bible. I'm not saying you should buy a new Bible; but plainly put you should start reading the word of God on a regular basis.

You know I didn't want you to feel like I've just added another list of things to do in Christ. Some of you may be saying, "Yeah right, I should walk in my purpose. I'll start today. No, don't shift into works mode, like most of us are prone to do. It's more about your decision; then confirming those decisions with your actions and allowing the Holy Spirit to help you with it all.

So I encourage you to change your perspective, raise your expectancy level and believe. Even, say it aloud, "I believe our Lord wants me to walk in my purpose and have a happy ending. Therefore, I raise my expectancy level to receive God's will for every area of my life."

Strengthening Your Step

Five Destiny Thieves Sent To Devour Your Destiny

The thief's purpose is to steal and kill and destroy. My purpose is to give them a rich and satisfying life. —John 10:10

A young pastor and his wife were destined to be happy parents of five, share their gift of love with the congregation and the world. Tragically, the husband began to drink. The more he drank the more violent he became.

After years of violence and bitterness, merely traces of their destiny remained. They might have fulfilled their destiny, if they had only known about the destiny thieves of bad company and the generational lies sent to steal their happy ending.

She was so proud of her children. She, like many mothers she knew had given her all to raise her children. She had the support of her parents who lived next door, her big sister and husband down the street and even the support of her neighbors who lived on either side of her.

Yet, she lacked the support of a spouse. She was a divorcee who raised six children, five boys and one girl. She might have fulfilled more of her destiny, if she had only known about the destiny thief of un-forgiveness sent to douse her passion and steal her destiny.

Have you encountered a set of circumstances that seemed designed to pervert or destroy your destiny? Maybe, it even succeeded for a season. Did it make you better or bitter? No need to answer that. Just know if it did, you don't have to stay that way.

Father God will help you, just ask. If not, how do we stay on track and help our children stay on track? Here are five destiny thieves sent to destroy your dreams. Through Christ, you can be victorious against any destiny thief. You can keep going recovering or overcoming all:

1. Bad company corrupts good character. Guard against staying connected with friends that don't share your values and desire to please God with a life of faith and purpose. Father God commanded us to come out from among them. We have to be holy (consecrated) as He is holy. If you don't select your friends well, you may find yourself headed for a destiny detour.

2. Open doors of sin will pervert God's destiny. Repent of any known sin in your life. Keep a repentive heart toward God, ready to repent of revealed sin. Be filled God's Holy Spirit, who was sent as a paracletos to convict us and lead us to repentance.

3. Unforgiveness that turns into bitterness. Harboring un-forgiveness will destroy the chances of you walking fully in your destiny and purpose. For un-forgiveness blocks the blessing of God from flowing in your life. Left unchecked, it turns into bitterness. Bitterness becomes a root that grows up and defiles many. If you discover or know you have un-forgiveness, repent and allow Father God to heal you. He's faithful and just to forgive us and cleanse us of all unrighteousness.

4. Generational curses, undetected, will seek to pull the plug on your destiny. Undisturbed and uncontested generational curses will certainly steal your destiny, if allowed. The good news is Christ has already redeemed us from any curse, but it has to be appropriated.

5. Giants in the land, roaring obscenities to the warriors of your family are looking to devour destinies. There are many things that can become giants in our lives throughout the families and generations. No matter, who or what they are, they can be overcome through Christ and by the Spirit of the Lord.

Facing a giant in your family that you are ready to get rid of forever. Pray and seek the Lord for strategy. For more on this topic, see WOW! Women of Legacy – Chapter Three Overcoming The Giants Of Your Generation.

Stay alert, the devil is as a roaring lion, seeking whom he may devour. Many families are perishing for lack of knowledge. For more on breaking generational curses, see WOW! Women of Legacy. Visit, Earma at http://wowontheweb.com

Crossroads

Continue Walking In Faith And Victory

But as for you, continue in what you have learned and firmly believed. You know those who taught you, and you know that from childhood you have known the sacred Scriptures, which are able to give you wisdom for salvation through faith in Christ Jesus. All Scripture is inspired by God and is profitable for teaching, for rebuking, for correcting, for training in righteousness... —2 Timothy 3:14,15,16

Are you still going strong? You know Jesus said first to the Jews and now to us who believe, "If you continue in My Word, you will truly become my disciples." So, it's an important question. I remember when the inscription was really popular 'Finish Strong.' It reminded us of the need to finish with all your might. And sometimes it seems to take all your might to finish well.

Today, I encourage you to continue in faith and producing the fruit of righteousness. Congratulations on getting started pursuing your destiny through serving. Now you must continue to the end. Finishing is even better than starting. Here's one thing that will help you finish strong in the kingdom of God.

Remember, all Scripture is inspired by God and is useful to teach us what is true and to make us realize what is wrong in our lives. It corrects us when we are wrong and teaches us to do what is right. With that in mind, let me tell you briefly about my experience with the Holy Spirit teaching me this principle.

Feeding Our Inner Man

He instructed me, feeding my inner man was similar to feeding my outer or physical man. That next day I obeyed the Holy Spirit's leading; I went and got a Daily-Reading-Bible to help get me in the habit. That was over twenty years ago, I'm still on the journey of reading my Bible daily to grow and stay strong, walking in faith and victory.

Don't get me wrong, I'm not trying to get you to do a religious act or add to the list you have to DO in Christ. You don't have to go out and buy a new Bible or even get a special one that's formatted to read daily.

But I am encouraging you in the way to build up your most holy faith in Christ and most importantly a relationship with your Father God. I firmly believe we grow spiritually by reading, meditating, studying and confessing the word of God more and more.

Remember, our weapons are not carnal but mighty to pulling down the strongholds of the enemy. They're not carnal but they are weapons; the word of God is a spiritual weapon. Ephesians 6 So, wherever you are in this process under the Holy Spirit's guidance as an armorbearer and servant leader, you should at least begin reading the Word of God as the Holy Spirit has instructed you to do.

Lots of us, Christians don't realize it's that simple yet it's that important as well. None of us would dream of not feeding the physical man for weeks, months and even years for some, surviving on one Sunday meal a week.

Yet, we somehow expect to go conquer spiritual giants and lands without our weapons and no spiritual diet and discipline...O.k., don't get me started. I don't mean to fuss. I want you to realize how important this is in serving and even your day to day success as a Christian.

⌘

Living Destiny and Fulfilling A God Given Purpose

By now, you might be wondering why I'm discussing all of this. It's because you'll need your spiritual strength to accomplish the task, God has assigned you to serve in His kingdom. You'll need to be established, strong and immovable to conquer every challenge and road block sent to discourage you, detour you and even cause you to give up on your divine destiny.

I don't know if you've noticed yet. But the moment you decide to go for it with all your might you come on the radar of another camp. When you decide I'm going to live my destiny and fulfill my God given purpose, you become a target of our enemy, the devil.

Walking In Faith And Victory

A young couple told me when they volunteered on the prison ministry team, they were overjoyed. But when it came to attending a weekly prayer and prep meeting, they would often get in a fight or get headaches right before the meeting.

They confessed they had to up their prayer and time in the word of God to get past it. For them, it didn't mean they never came under attack again but any opposition sent their way became far and fewer between.

They began to understand how to push past it through prayer and get stronger through the word of God to the point they could ignore it and go anyway.

So if you've been asking Father God to strengthen you and help you live a big life in Christ, keep serving, keep praying and spending time in the word of God and He will grow you.

To walk in faith and victory, follow His leading, His prompting, abide in the Vine. Do it this way (His way) and you can be sure you will safely arrive at your divine destiny.

Spotlight

15 Reasons Why Jesus Came And Your Big Purpose

Even as the Son of man came not to be ministered unto, but to minister, and to give his life a ransom for many. —Matthew 20:28

Throughout the Bible, its proclaimed why Jesus came to the earth. Some strategic reasons were proclaimed by Jesus, himself. I love it when that happened. Here are fifteen wonderful reasons Jesus came, why God sent you his daughter and your BIG purpose, in essence your mandate from God for what you are called to do:

1. Jesus Christ came into the world to save sinners.

"This is a faithful saying, and worthy of all acceptation, that Christ Jesus came into the world to save sinners; of whom I am chief." 1 Timothy 1:15,

2. Jesus came to call sinners to repentance. I love when I read Jesus proclaimed his purpose. He said himself, he came into the world to call sinners to repentance.

"When Jesus heard it, he saith unto them, They that are whole have no need of the physician, but they that are sick: I came not to call the righteous, but sinners to repentance." Mark 2:17,

3. Jesus Christ came to seek and save the lost. Without doubt, it was his mission.

"For the Son of man is come to seek and to save that which was lost." Luke 19:10,

4. Jesus came into the world to show the true purpose of life and give Himself as a ransom. It was demonstrated.

"Even as the Son of man came not to be ministered unto, but to minister, and to give his life a ransom for many." Matthew 20:28,

5. Jesus Christ came into the world to be a King and bear witness to the truth. He is royalty.

"Pilate therefore said unto him, Art thou a king then? Jesus answered, Thou sayest that I am a king. To this end was I born, and for this cause came I into the world, that I should bear witness unto the truth. Every one that is of the truth heareth my voice." John 18:37,

6. Jesus Christ came into the world to do the Will of His Father.

"For I came down from heaven, not to do mine own will, but the will of him that sent me." John 6:38,

7. Jesus Christ came into the world to be a Light in the world.

"I am come a light into the world, that whosoever believeth on me should not abide in darkness." John 12:46,

8. Jesus Christ came into the world that men might have the Abundant Life.

"I am come that they might have life, and that they might have it more abundantly." John 10:10,

9. Jesus Christ came into the world to Judge the world.

"And Jesus said, For judgment I am come into this world, that they which see not might see; and that they which see might be made blind." John 9:39,

10. Jesus Christ came into the world to Proclaim or preach the Good News about the Kingdom of God.

"And he said unto them, Let us go into the next towns, that I may preach there also: for therefore came I forth." Mark 1:38,

11. Jesus Christ came into the world to die on the cross.

"Now is my soul troubled; and what shall I say? Father, save me from this hour: but for this cause came I unto this hour." John 12:27,

12. Jesus Christ came into the world to fulfil the law.

"Think not that I am come to destroy the law, or the prophets: I am not come to destroy, but to fulfil." Matthew 5:17,

13. Jesus Christ came into the world to be a Divider of men.

"Think not that I am come to send peace on earth: I came not to send peace, but a sword. For I am come to set a man at variance against his father, and the daughter against her mother, and the daughter in law against her mother in law." Matthew 10:34, 35 (Christ makes it necessary to choose between relatives and the truth. This choice often causes division.)

14. Jesus Christ came into the world as a demonstration of God's Love.

"Herein is love, not that we loved God, but that he loved us, and sent his Son to be the propitiation for our sins." 1 John 4:10,

15. Jesus Christ came into the world because the Father sent Him.

"Then said Jesus to them again, Peace be unto you: as my Father hath sent me, even so send I you." May God bless you and make his face shine upon you, your family and ministry. John 20:21,

As you know, our purpose in God is directly related to the full purpose of why the Father sent Jesus. I discovered each story of recompense in the Bible had a larger themed thread in it. For Joan of Arc, Rahab, Ruth, Sarah, Candi Lightner, Florence Nightingale to Esther in the next chapter, it's always about the BIGGER picture.

With Joan of Arc, it was the French nation at stake. With Rahab, it was her role in saving her family, a nation and the birthing of Christ through the family line. Sarah, wife of Abraham and Ruth, the wife of Boaz, it was the same burden to share in faith that would that would impact, the world even humanity.

Candi Lightner and those who have risen up behind her example. They have changed our nation and the laws that impact people who choose to drive while drunk. And remember, Florence Nightingale, who became one of the founders of modern day nursing, as we know it. Countless lives were saved and impacted in hospitals on the other side of her finding her purpose.

So, whether your destiny and success is tied to the world-changing children you are raising, the school girls and boys you are mentoring, the neighborhood and community you are pastoring, it's always about, what I call your BIG purpose. So, don't get stuck on the 'why me' pity party. Raise your eyes to your BIG purpose tied to the mission and heart of God through Christ and go forth!

Summary

She was a pastor's wife with a gift of love destined to be God's minister of reconciliation. Tragically, the husband began to drink. After years of violence and bitterness, merely traces of their destiny remained. They might have fulfilled their destiny if they had only known about the destiny thieves sent to steal their happy ending. For me, it was worth the visit to remember how to guard against the destiny thieves.

I was reminded and hope you were too, whether your destiny and success is tied to the children you are raising, the school girls and boys you are mentoring, the neighborhood and community you are pastoring, it's always about, what I call your BIG purpose. So, don't get stuck on the 'why me' pity party. Raise your eyes to your BIG purpose tied to the mission and heart of God through Christ and go forth!

Destiny Challenge

Symbolic Illustration: Plug an appliance into an electrical outlet. See that it just works. Reflect on how we as Christians plug into our source. We abide in the vine. Talk about how we must stay connected to our sources. Jesus is the Way, the Truth and the Life.

Chapter Eight

Leaving A Legacy

A Woman's Pattern Of Power

And the king loved Esther and she found favor beyond all the other women, so he put on her the queen's crown. —Esther 2:17

A little girl was born in a time of turmoil for Israel. She was an orphan with no future and no destiny. Or so it seemed, what happened next could have changed her future and the generations to come. But Esther learned a secret that brought salvation to her nation with an unexpected upset of her enemies' plans so powerful that it echoes through the centuries.

Esther was a distinctive young woman. One of the translations of Esther means 'star.' Esther emerged as a star of her generation and left a legacy of leadership, godliness, selflessness and walking in her newly received royalty with grace and compassion. She faced the circumstances of her birth as an orphan and position with courage and hope. She was an obedient and highly favored young woman prepared for her Kairos moment, a night of destiny with the king.

In part Esther's story began, When the time was fulfilled for Esther daughter of Amina dab, the brother of Mordecai's father, to go in to the king, she neglected none of the things that Gai, the eunuch in charge of the women, had commanded. Now Esther found favor in the eyes of all who saw her.

So Esther went in to King Artaxerxes in the twelfth month, which is Adar, in the seventh year of his reign. And the king loved Esther and she found favor beyond all the other virgins, so he put on her the queen's diadem.

Sign Post to Destiny

YOU Are A Shining Star!

Those who are wise will shine like the brightness of the heavens, and those who lead many to righteousness, like the stars for ever and ever. —Daniel 12:3

Esther, an orphan rose to the full potential of her name, sometimes translated as 'star.' Her fame propelled her to the highest position of any woman in her day. Even through biblical history, her legacy and example reaches through the generations. Like Esther, regardless of our status in life, we are called to be a shining star, leaving a legacy of a life well lived.

Years ago, for a season the Holy Spirit would pull a certain set of words up in my spirit. I would wake up with the jingle in my mind and heart, "You are a shining star..." but couldn't remember the words. Fortunately, my husband Varn, a musician from childhood has a talent for remembering almost all the songs he hears and have heard. That in itself is amazing to me. This song was no different.

You're a shining star, no matter who you are— Shining bright to see what you can truly be—You're a shining star no matter who you are— Shining bright to see what you can truly be... Let me tell a cautionary tale, so to speak. I'm not endorsing this group. For they were a secular music group. Since, the Holy Spirit used it to prompt me in this teaching, I'm giving you a little background and history, even though you probably don't need it. (smile)

"Shining Star" is a 1975 song by Earth, Wind & Fire from their album That's the Way of the World. The song was written by Maurice White, Larry Dunn and Philip Bailey and produced by White. "Shining Star" was Earth, Wind & Fire's first major hit, hitting No. 1 on both the U.S. Hot 100 and R&B charts.

In 1975, Earth, Wind & Fire The Shining Star song hit the charts at U.S. Billboard Hot 100 at #1. Shining Star" won Earth, Wind & Fire a Grammy for Best R&B Performance by a Duo or Group with Vocals.

The little snippet of the song served as a thread that I followed to the word of God to see what he says about us being stars. It became a prophetic riddle in my life. I hope it does for you too. Here are a couple scripture notes that say we are called to be shining stars in God's kingdom:

1. Those who are wise will shine like the brightness of the heavens, and those who lead many to righteousness, like the stars for ever and ever. — Daniel 12:3

2. And the teachers and those who are wise shall shine like the brightness of the firmament, and those who turn many to righteousness (to uprightness and right standing with God) [shall give forth light] like the stars forever and ever. —Daniel 12:3 (AMP)

3. So that no one can criticize you. Live clean, innocent lives as children of God, shining like bright stars in a world full of crooked and perverse people. —Philippians 2:15

4. "You are the light of the world. A town built on a hill cannot be hidden. —Matthew 5:14

Now that we know we are called to be stars for Jesus, here are six confessions to memorize, meditate, and speak over yourself and others.

1. I am a shining star for Jesus. May any fame I attain reflect Christ to a dark world. "So that no one can criticize you. Live clean, innocent lives as children of God, shining like bright stars in a world full of crooked and perverse people." —Philippians 2:15

2. I radiate light wherever I go. "You are the light of the world. A town built on a hill cannot be hidden." —Matthew 5:14

3. I shine like a firework in the night. "Then you will shine among them like stars in the sky." —Philippians 2:15

4. **I am a daughter of Light.** "You are all children of the light and children of the day. We do not belong to the night or to the darkness." —1 Thessalonians 5:5

5. **I am the salt of the earth.** "You are the salt of the earth." —Matthew 5:13

6. **I am a vessel of His Light.** "For God, who said, "Let light shine out of darkness," made his light shine in our hearts to give us the light of the knowledge of God's glory displayed in the face of Christ." —2 Corinthians 4:6

7. **Beams and light and joy exude from within me.** "Light shines on the godly, and joy on those whose hearts are right." —Psalm 97:11

After you embrace your self-worth, your beauty and joy in Christ, you have the fearlessness and fierceness to step into your destiny and reign… For more affirmations and declarations, visit http://wowontheweb.com for the WOW! Women Manifesto.

A Step toward Destiny

God's Story Of Recompense

For the LORD has a day of vengeance, a year of recompense for Zion's cause. Isaiah 34:8

Esther's story in part, continues with Father God's intervention as Jehovah Gmolah, the Lord of Recompense. Through Esther's faith and perseverance, along with Mordecai and the nation of Israel God told the story of recompense. The prevailing story resounds through the generations.

Father God proclaims, "Vengeance is mine, I always recompense. The Roman writer confirms his words, "Beloved, never avenge yourselves, but leave it to the wrath of God, for it is written, 'Vengeance is mine, I will repay, says the Lord.'" —Romans 12:9

On that note, have you noticed Father God takes up for His people? He wants you to know, He not only has your back; He has a payback designed just for you. I've learned God doesn't waste any of our pain or troubles. He's a God that compensates and even repays you for your works, good or bad. Prophet Jeremiah declares, "For the Lord is the God of recompense. He will surely repay." (Jer. 51:56)

I've discovered recompense is one of the laws of the kingdom of God. Remember, the sowing and reaping law. I think we (the Body of Christ) and the world are familiar with this one by now. You know what goes around, comes around. What you sow, you shall reap. So, it is with His vengeance and His recompense. Hey, you didn't say anything about vengeance.

Yeah, I know but they go hand in hand. Father God said, "Vengeance is Mine. And I always recompense. So, it's important for you to know or remember that you don't have to hate. You don't have to get even.

Like I said, God's got your back. Just keep on forgiving when someone wrongs you. But watch what God does. It's God's way to trouble those that trouble you... But I'm getting a little ahead of myself. I don't want to miss the foundation I'm about to lay so let me back up.

Going back to the story of Cain and Abel, we see the law of recompense in effect. It was the law of recompense that demanded justice for Abel's right sacrifice and his wrongful death. Many of you know how this story ends. Just in case you are new to the stories of the Bible, Abel offered right sacrifice and Cain offered sacrifice that was not pleasing to God.

Cain murdered his brother Abel. God judged Cain for his sin and wrong actions. Apart from Adam and Eve, it's one of the first pictures of recompense and retribution. Even so, I encourage you to read the story of Cain and Abel with fresh eyes and with the law of recompense in mind.

Years ago, as a new Christian I went through a season of extremely troubling circumstances. I was severely persecuted on my job by my boss. One day, after a meeting with other managers, the others were filing out laughing and talking.

He walked up to me and whispered, "You should pack your bags now. Start looking for another job because I'm going to make sure you quit." I was shocked. That afternoon, I was in an accident. A drunk driver ran into the rear end of my car.

It sent me and my vehicle into a tail spin, like a spinning top. All I could do was hold on to the steering wheel. My car stopped within inches of the big picture window of a nearby restaurant. The people ran out and delivered me from the drunk driver. He had climbed out of his car, fussing and wagging his finger at me for driving in front of him on a red light. The truth was, I had no idea. My mind was still reeling from the words my manager had just whispered to me.

He made my job and life miserable. But with God's help, I never quit. When I came through this season, I was grateful. But because of lack of wisdom and understanding about God, I felt hurt, abandoned and disappointed that He had not intervened and taken me out of this unwarranted trouble.

Instead, I was allowed to go through and suffered great loss. (Sound familiar?) I kept going over the scenes and episodes in my mind. Until finally one day in a vision He showed me the exact repayment of troubles my enemies had received. I woke up with the words in my spirit from God, "I always recompense!"

For me, that day my journey began with learning about God's recompense, even His law of recompense. I had never heard the word recompense used to apply to anything in my natural world. No one had said to me, "I recompense you." To help expand our understanding of God's recompense, Webster defines it to mean: to repay or reward; to compensate as in a loss, etc.

Not long ago, Father God said to me, "The Days of Recompense have come." Knowing God gifts us with many different seasons, I immediately began to think about what He has taught me over the years about His recompense. My heart was stirred in faith and expectancy about this season of God's recompense.

I want to share a little of it now. So, you can begin to look around with the same hope and expectancy of what God is doing in our life as Christian women. Perhaps you'll find that he has been speaking to you already about the same thing. If not, I have good news!

If you've been going through troubles and especially unwarranted trouble, you can expect God's recompense. You have a payback, even a compensation coming. Here's five things I've learned about God's law of recompense:

1. The law of recompense? I call it a law because He said, "I always recompense." In Scripture, just like his other laws it's applied to the just and unjust. Remember, God is a good god. He rains on the just and the unjust. His sun shines on the obedient and the disobedient. Recompense and retribution are applied to every man, the just and the unjust. It is up to us (humanity), whether we receive reward, benefits and protection or penalties, punishments and judgments. (Proverbs 11:31)

2. Two sides to recompense? Even though recompense is applied to every man, there are two sides of recompense and retribution. One side is reward and the other is punishment. Rev. Brown wrote it so eloquently, "As long as we are in obedience to His Word, we receive the benefits and protection (rewards) of God's law of recompense. But when we are living in disobedience, we inadvertently open to the judgments and even punishments of the law." (Proverbs 12:13,1)

3. The battle is the Lord's? I've learned if you want to receive God's recompense, you can't get out there and fight for yourself. If you've been wrongfully troubled, accused, mistreated you must forgive and allow Father God to fight the battle. Don't hold a hateful grudge; walk in forgiveness and know revenge belongs to God. The writer of Romans said it like this, "Avenge not yourselves, beloved, but give place unto the wrath of God; for it is written, Vengeance belongeth unto me; I will recompense, saith the Lord." (Rom. 12:19)

4. Will God remember to recompense? Many have asked, myself included, "Why so long to recompense?" First of all, God is sovereign. Meaning His timing is perfect. I'm glad He's God and I'm not. In general, I'm glad man is not in charge of such things. The Apostle Peter said it well, "The Lord is not slack concerning His promise, as some count slackness, but is longsuffering toward us, not willing that any should perish but that all should come to repentance." (2 Peter 3:9) The writer of Hebrews puts it another way, "For God is not unjust to forget your work and labor of love which you have shown toward His name, in that you have ministered to the saints and do minister." (Hebrews 6:10)

5. Recompense by Faith? There is no room for boasting. None of us can say, hey I've done everything right so recompense me God. Remember, all of us only entered in right relationship with God through Christ. The shed blood of Christ ultimately satisfied the requirements of God's justice (law of recompense).

In other words, you can shout right here! When you accepted Christ into your heart, you made a covenant with God. You are in right relationship with Him and eligible for His promises of recompense. His recompense includes working all things to your good.

It means He will not waste a drop of your pain and troubles. Just as He did Job, he will pay you back double. Just like Mordecai, He will be careful to honor and exalt you in due season. Because you share in Christ suffering, the law of recompense says you share in His glory.

And just like he proclaimed to me, when we've been treated unjustly, he always recompenses. It has not escaped his attention. Since, our thoughts and ways are not like God's we don't always understand. But you can be sure he has purpose in just intentions for your life. His plans are for your good. He plans an expected end, even a bright future ahead for you. So, don't lose hope. Look to the hills from whence your help comes from.

As the Holy Spirit begins to point to examples of recompense around you, my hope is that your faith begins to grow to receive all that God has reserved for you. You can look for it; expect it and receive God's recompense by faith.

Strengthening Your Step

A Pattern To Follow

Esther's actions left a pattern of courage and loyalty to her people that we can take example from. The Bible book Esther named after her is one of the few books dedicated to a story with a woman as the main character. Many researchers and scholars have said, it was not intended to be there.

According to them, it was deemed a novella, therefore, it was only by accident that it appears in the modern day translated Bibles. That may or may not be so, I'm just thankful it made it. I suspect it was Father God's plan all along. He loves confounding the wise with so called foolishness. Besides, it's a wonderful story of His recompense.

Have you created something using a pattern? You know; did you use a template or a blueprint to make it easier. Most everyone enjoys using a template to jumpstart their creations. My mother used patterns to sew clothing and quilts when my sisters, brothers and I were children.

I remember sitting by her side and watching her unfold the patterns, laying them out on the table or floor. Then she would carefully study and cut each piece of cloth to make sure it was measured exactly to the specs of the pattern. It was a joy to see her finished products of dresses, suits and beautiful quilts.

Perhaps, its why I use patterns even now in my life in various ways. I use patterns, systems, templates, recipes, formulas to make my life easier. I love them. It often gives me the jumpstart I need to get things done quickly in excellence. I realized a long time ago, I can't be a master at everything. Therefore, to shorten my learning curve when I don't have the time to master a task or don't want to master it. I look for an easy template to jumpstart my work.

Not long ago, I discovered God uses patterns in our lives. Remember, all of humanity was started with the creation of one man and woman. Yes, we are created uniquely and wonderfully but in a similar pattern to Adam and Eve. And now just as importantly, he expects us to become more and more a pattern to other believers.

The Apostle Paul in a letter to the Philippians' believers encouraged them to pattern their lives after him and take note of others that lived up to his example.[1] Then again, he encourages Pastor Timothy and now us with his words, "Hold tightly to the pattern of truth I taught you, especially concerning the faith and love of Jesus Christ offers you. Guard well the splendid, God given ability you received as a gift from the Holy Spirit who lives within you."[2]

Through the Apostle Paul and other Scripture writers, God commands us to pattern our lives after those who have ran their race well and now have gone on before us. Lately, I've been examining what kind of legacy I'm leaving or even what kind of example am I living in the now? I want to make sure I'm laying a good and worthy pattern for the believers in my circle.

How about you, dear friend? Are you a good example for your family and those in your circle of influence? Won't you join me in laying a good pattern of diligence, of being a good soldier enduring hardships of the season, making ourselves content in whatever circumstance we face or enjoy. Link arms with me in showing ourselves as a hard worker, training for excellence in communicating the gospel and as a patient farmer in the Kingdom of God sowing and reaping in due season. —Philippians 3:17

Crossroads

Returning To Our First Love

Have you realized when you drift away from God, you always stay longer than you anticipated and you go further than you ever thought you would go?

That's exactly what happened to me as a teenager. I loved to read Bible stories as a five-year-old. There was a prayer of salvation at the back of the book. I prayed it and received Christ at an early age. Then, as a teen-ager, I walked away from God and said I'll be back. In Christianese, you could say I back-slid.

I won't go into it but I can tell you my life took a downward spiral after that. You veteran Christians know the result of that decision. Anyway, on with my story.

First Love

Twenty-four years later, in 1987 I was a discount retail manager in the New Orleans and Louisiana area. I got promoted and my company moved me to the Gulf Coast of Mississippi. I was so excited that I would be living a few miles from the ocean. Little did I know something bigger than that was brewing; my life was about to change forever.

One of my fellow managers in the area started to talk to me about God. I had already spouted out that he could talk to me about God but no preaching. I told him I hadn't listened to any preaching in over fifteen years and I wasn't about to start now.

He kept talking anyway. Sometimes, I would get up and leave. One day through a word of knowledge he said, "Father God said he wants you back. You said you would be back. He says he wants you back. Then he began to tell me a story. It was a story I read over and over again as a child. I read it scores of times.

He went on to say, "He says you'll recognize this story." He started to tell me the story of Saul of Tarsus who became Paul the Apostle. He reminded me of how Saul was busy breathing out threats and persecution of the Christians. And how a light shone from heaven blinded him and knocked him from his horse…Of course, after reading it nearly a hundred times I remembered immediately. I jumped up and said, "You're scaring me now. No one could know those things about me."

Later that night, I began to think about what happened. I began to wonder how it would be being back with the Lord. Could it even happen? Hadn't I gone too far to ever be retrieved, to ever change? The rest is history. Weeks later, when I saw my friend again I was ready. He led me in a prayer. I recommitted my life to God. I accepted Christ as my Lord and Savior.

When Did You Commit To Christ

Which brings me to the question I have for you. Do you remember when you committed to Christ? Were you a youngster, a middle aged adult or did you make a serious commitment, recently? Either way, you might consider marking that day; you know write it down, even memorializes it.

Why? Because you may need to refer to it along the way. When it gets tough or you get weary, it can be inspiration—food for your journey. At last, you need to pass it to the next generation. When they ask why is that day so special to you—you can tell them about your decision for Christ and what it means to you.

Remember the Israelites, Father God periodically would have them create a memorial for something. For example, when they first crossed the Jordan River into the Promised Land he commanded them to have twelve priests each select a stone from the river bed and create a memorial on the bank.

They created a twelve stone memorial so that when their children would ask about it, they could tell the story of how God as a shepherd brought his people from Egypt into the Promised Land.

I'm serious; if you can't mark a day, a year or even a season when you first believed or your heart was changed for Christ, you might need to return to your first love. Do an X marks the spot—I first committed my life to Christ. Go over your story once again. Write down or record your testimony, at least tell it to someone afresh. Give them the short version. Don't overload but do give it.

First Volunteered

There's another decision I want to talk to you about, for the same reason. Here's the question. Do you remember when you first decided to serve God in your local church? When was the first time you volunteered in church or served on the Usher, Hospitality team or Children's ministry? Or in our case, when did you become a Servant Leader?

Remember the first things. Think about how excited you were to do the things of God. Consider why you do what you do? Did you realize it was God prompting you, leading you to do what you do?

I remember back in Mississippi, my pastor asked me to help count the offerings on Sunday and serve on an accounting team that met once a week to take care of church business. I was new in the church and didn't agree at first. To be honest, I had some wrong ideas about serving in church. I already worked long hours on my job. So in my mind why should I do that with no expectation of pay? But willing to change, I asked God what he thought about it.

It Is God At Work In You

Our friend and advocate the Holy Spirit spoke these simple words of Scripture to me, "...for it is God who is at work in you, both to will and to work for His good pleasure." –Philippians 2:13b

On through the years, it has been the source of my zeal—my relationship with Christ and His command through the Holy Spirit and Scripture that it is Him working through us all (as we allow Him) to do His will and good pleasure.

I've served in many different capacities by His leading and eventually became a servant leader that our books and ministry were birthed from. You can read more of our servant leadership story in our latest book 'In The Spirit of Leadership by Varn Brown.

In closing, I encourage you to return to your first love and mark it. Even create a memorial, a testimony to encourage you when you're weary in the battle. And above all to pass it to the next generation. Stir up the zeal of God to do His will! The Hebrew writer said it best, "who saved us and called us to a holy calling not because of our works but because of his own purpose and grace which he gave us in Christ Jesus before the ages began." —2 Timothy 1:9

Spotlight

7 Ways To Live Your Legacy

Let each generation tell its children of your mighty acts; let them proclaim your power. —Psalm 145:4

Are you designing your life as a torch? With your eye on the next generation, you've decided, no matter what, you want to live your life well as an example. There's good news! You can live a life of legacy. God is a god of the generations.

He is the same yesterday, today and forever. Through God's plan, this generation prepares and passes the torch to the next. Inside this third book of the WOW! Women series, you will discover seven steps on how to prepare and live your life as a legacy:

1. **Leaving A Legacy for Generations To Come:** A Woman's Pattern Of Power. We begin our new study with Esther, a shining star of her generation. Her fame and legacy still make a great pattern for us to follow.

2. **Tapping Into Your Inner Queen**: A Woman's Royal Call To Rule. Queen of Sheba and her entourage arrived in Israel to visit King Solomon to

further her education and receive what was valued above silver and gold. She came bearing elephantine piles of gifts to honor and gain access to wisdom, knowledge and insight beyond what she could ask or imagine...

3. Breaking The Generational Curses: A Woman's War With Words. Learn the power of life and death in your words. Discover how to break the curse running rampant through the generations of your family.

4. Overcoming the Giants of Your Generation: A Woman's Will To Win. Re-discover the power of choice and a will to win. Find out how to overcome the giants of your generations, once and for all.

5. Preparing the Torch of Legacy: A Woman's Torch Of Legacy. Study how to prepare your life as a torch to be passed.

6. Living the Legacy: A Woman's Life Well Lived. Discover how to live your life as a legacy to pass to the next generation.

7. THRIVE: A discipleship and mentorship program for WOW! Women all over the world. See how to join, make your mark and pass it on. http://wowwomenglobal.com

"Father God desires the same for each generation. God said to Moses, "I AM WHO I AM"; and He said, "Thus you shall say to the sons of Israel, 'I AM has sent me to you.'" God, furthermore, said to Moses, "Thus you shall say to the sons of Israel, 'The LORD, the God of your fathers, the God of Abraham, the God of Isaac, and the God of Jacob, has sent me to you.' This is My name forever, and this is My memorial-name to all generations. Exodus 3:14,15

Father God has put in each of us a blueprint, the thoughts, plans and desire for a bright future," explains Earma. "I have designed the WOW! Women message to hopefully position the reader to receive God's plans to satisfy that longing," Start your journey today using the seven lessons in everything you do and experience the joy of creating a life full of passion, purpose and power in God then leaving a legacy of a life well-lived.

Summary

Have realized YOU are a shining star? A little girl was born in a time of turmoil for Israel. She was an orphan with no future and no destiny. Or so it seemed, what happened next could have changed her future and the generations to come. But Esther learned a secret that brought salvation to her nation with an unexpected upset of her enemies' plans so powerful that it echoes through the centuries.

Esther embraced her preparation season and followed the instructions from her mentors to the letter. It worked and she was ready for her Kairos season. She even discovered the real reason for her journey, to save a people.

She used every ounce of her skill, discernment, wisdom, knowledge and all that had prepared her for such a time as this. She stepped out in faith, prayed, fasted and received miraculous strategy to war against the evil intent of Israel's foes.

Yet none of it would have done any good, if she hadn't taken the courage to act. Through the generations, we take example from a woman who rose to stardom, even royalty from the meager beginnings of an orphan.

Destiny Challenge

Prepare a journal of life's lessons; write down at least five to ten. Get another copy of this book or all three books. Find someone at least one generation removed from yours and give these items to them. It can be your daughter, a niece, or a younger cousin. Put a note inside one of the books explaining the reasons you did this. Ask them to do the same, when they grow up.

Summary

In *Chapter One Going To Your Destiny* - A Woman's Predestination, I posed the question: Have you wanted your happy ending? The destiny seed of your future; God has put it in your heart, already. You didn't make it up. The seed that the Prophet Jeremiah proclaimed to Old Testament Jews and now to us is still the same: God has planned for, thoughtfully initiated, and even designed a blueprint for our future. —Jeremiah 29:11

I was amazed and elated to see that so much of God's heart and enthusiasm was revealed through the three small words of plan, hope and future through that Scripture. Remember, plan was defined as thoughts (not only thoughts but thoughtfulness and care), blueprint, direction or purpose.

Hope was explained as your expectancy of good, your faith, your dream, an expected good end and even your destination. The definitive word future pointed to God's plan for our chance to succeed, our due season, our final outcome, our fate or simply our destiny.

So, we can say with confidence God has a blueprint for our life. He has planned my destiny and I will receive my chance to succeed. I pray you were charged as I was with the knowledge that it is our responsibility to lay aside every weight and the sin that so easily besets us to run the race God has set before us.

I pray it was good news as it was to me to discover Father God's desire to give us a happy ending. Additionally, He wants us to have an awareness of our destiny that will cause every woman of God to turn to each other saying, "Now is the time! Go to your destiny!"

In *Chapter Two Walking Through The Process* - A Woman's Pursuit Of God's Presence Are you weary with waiting for your destiny to appear? You have been looking for your moment to arrive. Well, I have good news!

It's finally your time. God's words are no longer postponed or delayed. But the words He speaks are done.

All you have to do is receive it by faith. Now, you're eligible to join your faith with patience and receive the promise of God. Just like Rahab, a former Jerichoian prostitute, we have to take a step, a first step or a next step. You might be scared or you may feel a sudden peace.

Either way, now is the time. Look what happened for Rahab and others like her, including me. It meant so much to me when the Holy Spirit told me to do as Rahab did. I discovered her first step started the journey to her destiny. Eventually, it landed her in the Christian faith hall of fame, married to one of the spies, an honorable mention in the genealogy of Christ and changed her family's life forever?

The king and the whole city trembled in fear at news of the plans of the Israelis and their God. But Rehab alone confessed and believed, "Your God is God!" She stepped out and pursued God to save her entire family. And you know the story by now. God did it. He's doing it for me. And he will do it for you. See you next chapter. We've started the journey…

Next *Chapter Three was Seizing Your Season* - A Woman's Precocious Power Of Preparation Are you ready for your Kairos season? I learned working with the Holy Spirit, we each can be ready our God timed season of success.

To get started, get organized and develop a spirit of readiness. Simply put, it's get ready and stay ready. You may be like I was, when the Holy Spirit kept prompting me stay ready, Earma, stay ready. Your promise is imminent…

I was reminded that the promises are received through faith and patience. We receive what we believe now. But just like the ten virgins who awaited the Bridegroom, we await the promises of God to manifest and materialize in our life.

As we stay connected and led by God's Spirit, we can discern and know the seasons of life. In this chapter, we have been discussing our preparation season and how we can operate in a spirit of readiness and stay ready for God's Kairos opportunity and destiny.

Remember when you use patience, you are indeed developing a spirit of readiness. You will become like all the other Saints of God in the Bible and in our modern day, you will receive the promise through faith and patience.

With all that said, staying ready doesn't mean things will never change. Being ready may just mean staying ready to change, holding on lightly to the things of this world.

And cultivating a mind and heart ready to go with Jesus when He comes again. Or even just as importantly, staying ready to obey when He leads, prompts and directs you to your destiny.

Inside *Chapter Four Turning Your Troubles To Triumph* - A Woman's Fiery Passion Points To Purpose we considered if we were lit for a purpose? Candy Lightner, a normal housewife with children got mad after her twelve-year-old daughter, Cari was killed by a drunk driver.

She found herself in the midst of her destiny, which caused her to almost single-handedly change a nation's complacent thinking about drinking while driving? Armed with a passion to help other mothers face similar tragedies, she formed MADD (Mothers Against Drunk Driving) and in the process turned her troubles into triumphs.

I was grateful to be reminded to make lemonade out of my troubles. It made me ask myself the question I asked you in the chapter. What troubles do you have, waiting for you to use as fuel to your flame? Even, gently put, what mess can become your mission?

The efforts of that foundational group of MADD ultimately resulted in more than 360 chapters (still counting) throughout the world. A national commission against drunk driving has initiated more than 400 new laws in fifty states which address drunk driving.

Additionally, other organizations have caught the vision of making a difference. Groups such as (SADD) Students Against Drunk Driving and (PAAD) Performing Artist Against Drugs have joined the cause in their area of concern.

When Jesus walked this earth he had a passion for helping God's people and destroying the works of Satan. Indeed, Scripture says, "For this purpose was the Son of God made manifest." His passion led him to his purpose and destiny (1 John 3:8). Discover your passion it may lead you to your purpose!

Continuing with *Chapter Five Receiving Your Appointment From God* - A Woman's Wild Purpose Leads To Power. We discussed receiving your appointment from God? Florence Nightingale was born when it was not considered proper for a young woman to become a nurse. Her parents forbade it, society frowned upon it, and the medical professionals ignored it.

Yet, Florence Nightingale prepared her life and those she influenced. She was literally ready for her Kairos season. Through courage, skill and readiness, she changed the way the world viewed nursing and women.

Where did she begin? I was encouraged and delighted to discover she received her appointment from God. (I hope you were too!) She received her appointment in the garden of her parent's wealthy home in Yorkshire, New England.

She persevered through the persecution and antics sent by her family to defer her work in this field. It seemed the more determined they became, the more she forged forward to get training and stay prepared.

Prepared for what, you may have been asking. She didn't know her biggest challenges lay ahead. No one knew the Crimean War was in their future. But through preparation and training, she was able to rise to her Kairos season. Yes! I am still reeling from the fact that no one knew what to do with the horrific conditions in the military hospital before she arrived with her team.

Getting your appointment from God is the best advice you can ever receive. It's as simple as that. Ask him what your appointment is and he will show you. Remember Prophet Jeremiah instructed us with God's thoughts that are for our good, not for bad.

God thinks about the good and expected end he has in store for us. Keep it moving. Stay on the journey. Prepare for your Kairos season. It may take some time. But it will surely come; for He is faithful to keep his promises.

Moving forward with, *Chapter Six Praying Through To Power* - A Woman's Prayer And Propitious Power. Have you been clothed with power from above? The call of God and her destiny was wrapped up into the development of this virtue. After years of trial sent to help her develop it, Kathryn Kulhman became considered the beloved woman of God extraordinaire because of her faith, perseverance and relationship with the Holy Spirit.

In the biography of Ms. Kulhman, we discovered through it all, through failure, problems in her personal life and ministry, she persevered and found power with God. She went on to introduce the Holy Spirit to another generation in a way that had not been seen.

I was joyful to see the audacious power to ASK and the DIVINE YES emerge as one of the prominent revelations of this chapter. There came a fresh faith to ASK Father God for His promises. I remembered whatever we ask for according to his word, he hears us and if he hears we have what we've asked for.

Even while writing this book, I've suffered setbacks, disappointments and generally God's process in which I'm grateful for. I remembered Jesus explanation of Satan's true purpose to steal, kill and destroy along with his purpose embodied in his words, 'I came that you might have life more abundantly."

With that in mind, I was encouraged to dream again as I encouraged you to dream again. Finally, know that we serve a God of recompense, who is ready to give you your story of recompense.

Wrapping it up with *Chapter Seven Fulfilling Your Passion, Purpose And Power In God* - A Woman's Power To Propel Your Destiny. She was a pastor's wife with a gift of love destined to be God's minister of reconciliation. Tragically, the husband began to drink.

After years of violence and bitterness, merely traces of their destiny remained. They might have fulfilled their destiny if they had only known about the destiny thieves sent to steal their happy ending. For me, it was worth the visit to remember how to guard against the destiny thieves.

I was reminded and hope you were too, whether your destiny and success is tied to the children you are raising, the school girls and boys you are mentoring, the neighborhood and community you are pastoring, it's always about, what I call your BIG purpose.

So, don't get stuck on the 'why me' pity party. Raise your eyes to your BIG purpose tied to the mission and heart of God through Christ and go forth!

Finally, with Chapter Eight *Leaving A Legacy* - A Woman's Pattern of Power I sought to give you a preview of WOW! Women of Legacy. Have realized you are a shining star? A little girl was born in a time of turmoil for Israel. She was an orphan with no future and no destiny.

Or so it seemed, what happened next could have changed her future and the generations to come. But Esther learned a secret that brought salvation to her nation with an unexpected upset of her enemies' plans so powerful that it echoes through the centuries.

Esther embraced her preparation season and followed the instructions from her mentors to the letter. It worked and she was ready for her Kairos moment. She even discovered the real reason for her journey, to save a people. She used every ounce of her skill, discernment, wisdom, knowledge and all that had prepared her for such a time as this.

She stepped out in faith, prayed, fasted and received miraculous strategy to war against the evil intent of Israel's foes. Yet none of it would have done any good, if she hadn't taken the courage to act. Through the generations, we take example from a woman who rose to stardom, even royalty from the meager beginnings of an orphan.

Bibliography

- Joyce Meyers, The Confident Woman: Start Today Living Boldly And Without Fear (Warner Faith Hachette Book Group, 2006)
- Ann Spangler & Jean E. Syswerda, Women of the Bible, A One-Year Devotional Study of Women In Scripture (Zondervan Publishing House, 1999.)
- Sue and Larry Richards, Every Woman In The Bible, Fully Illustrated (Thomas Nelson Publishers, 1999.)
- Joyce Meyers, How to Succeed at Being Yourself: Finding the Confidence to Fulfill Your Destiny (Tulsa: Harrison House, 1999.)
- J.W. Martin (Compiled by), The Spirit-Filled Woman (Lake Mary: Creation House, 1997.)
- Elizabeth George, Beautiful in God's Eyes (Eugene: Harvest House Publishers, 1998.)
- Elizabeth George, A Woman After God's Own Heart (Eugene: Harvest House Publishers, 1995.)
- Laurie Beth Jones, Jesus CEO: Using Ancient Wisdom for Visionary Leadership (New York: Laurie Beth Jones, 1995.)
- Dr. Lester Sumrall, The Names of God: God's Name Brings Hope, Healing, and Happiness (New Kensington: Whitaker House, 1996.)
- Fred and Anna Kendall with Mary Hollingsworth, Speaking of Love: Learn the 7 Behavioral Life Languages of Highly Effective Communication (Dallas: Fred and Anna Kendall, 1995.)
- Joni Lamb, Surrender All: Your Answer to Living with Peace, Power & Purpose (Colorado Springs: Waterbrook Press, 2008.)
- Linda Weber, Woman of Splendor: Discovering the Four Facets of a Godly Woman (Nashville, Broadman & Holman Publishers, 1999.)

○ Carolyn Savelle, The Intensity of Your Desires, The Keys to Unlocking the Answers to Your Prayers (Crowley: Jerry Savelle Publications, 2000.)

○ Cynthia Heald, Becoming a Woman of excellence (Colorado Springs: NavPress, 2005.)

○ Cynthia Heald, Becoming a Woman of Prayer (Colorado Springs: NavPress, 2005.)

Discussion Guide

WOW! Women Of Destiny

Chapter One – Going To Your Destiny

1. In Chapter One of the WOW! Women of Destiny book, the author describes what she calls a destiny seed. What scripture is this concept based on? A powerful hint is; it can be found in the book of Jeremiah.

2. In chapter one, the author discussed how everyone encounters stumbling blocks in the race life. She named what she considers the five top stumbling blocks in the race called life. Name three stumbling blocks listed in the chapter.

3. The author also discussed seven assassins in the 'Signpost To Destiny' section sent to kill your dream, name at least three of these death threats usually sent to kill your dream, also listed in chapter one. Which one have you had to face and overcome in fulfilling your dream? Write out and memorize the scripture John 10:10 The thief comes only to steal and kill and destroy; I have come that they may have life, and have it to the full.

Chapter Two – Walking Through Your Process

4. From the table of contents chapter two, who was the featured heroine? What do you remember about her? Name one reason, why you think she was chosen as featured heroine in Chapter 2 A Woman's Pursuit of God's Presence?

5. In the Signpost To Destiny section the author outlines five ways to seek God's presence effectively; what are they? They all begin with seek:

1. Seek _____

2. Seek _____

3. Seek _____

4. Seek _____

5. Seek _____

6. In chapter two, also the author lays out seven powers God has given each of us to help us walk through any process he allows us to encounter. He always has blessing, promotion and reward on the other side. But to get to it we have to do like Jesus did, go through the process. The Bible says he endured the shame of the cross for the joy set before him…It's God's way that we go through the process. So, name the seven powers God has given us to help us make it through the process.

1. The Power of _____

2. The Power of _____

3. The Power of _____

4. The Power of _____

5. The Power of _____

6. The Power of _____

7. The Power of _____

6a. What do you remember about the author's acronym TRUST and submitting to God's process? Let me be clear Father God is faithful. He will not fail us or forsake us. So, here is our pattern to follow, we must submit to the process. Here are some suggestions formed into the acronym T.R.U.S.T. that will help us through the process.

Timing: _____

Recompense: _____

Understanding: _____

Sovereign: _____

Territory: _____

Chapter Three - Seizing Your Season

7. The author deliberately defines Kairos. Can you now define Kairos? If not, look it up in the dictionary and write below. The author told the reader about an eclectic group of twelve people were looking for their Kairos moment. What virtue did they all commonly need to obtain it? Write it below and how you are implementing in your life.

8. In chapter three, the author discussed the spirit of readiness and twenty-one ways to walk in it yourself? Write below, the three ways to walk in the spirit of readiness that stood out to you the most and why they are meaningful to you.

9. In the Strengthening Your Step section of chapter three, the author discussed carpe diem. What does this term mean, write below? After defining it, name one point from the author's discussion of six points. Why is this point meaningful to you?

Chapter Four - Turning Your Troubles Into Triumph

10. Write the theme scripture of Chapter Four below and briefly, what it means to you.

11. Who is the featured heroine in this chapter? Write her name below. What's the most important thing you've learned about her? Write it below, also.

12. The author proposes; our passions may be an indicator of God-given wow! women of destiny desires that must be directed by him. She gave the reader ten simple guidelines. Write below the top three that spoke to you the loudest.

12a. The author outlined 10 Passion Thieves Sent To Destroy Your Dreams to guard against. Pinpoint the three top thieves you've dealt with in your life. Write them below. What you are doing to make sure they don't steal your dreams.

Chapter Five - Receiving Your Purpose From God

13. What is the theme scripture for chapter five? Write it below and what it means to you.

14. Who is the featured heroine in chapter five? Write her name below. What's the most important thing you've learned about her? Write it below, also.

15. The author proposes that some things happen for the obedient believer that don't happen for the disobedient?

She wrote in the 'Strengthening Your Step: 7 Steps To Walking Out Your Purpose With God Through Service' section God is no respecter of persons but he does make a distinction between the obedient and disobedient.

Name three things that happen for the obedient believer that you are looking to see happen in your life. Write below.

Chapter Six – Praying Through To God's Power

16. What is the theme scripture for chapter six? Write it below and what it means to you.

17. Who is the featured heroine in chapter six? Write her name below. What's the most important thing you've learned about her? Write it below, also.

18. In the 'Signpost to Destiny: The Audacious Power of Ask, the author outlines five things to make sure you've asked for as a Christian. Write below the top three things you have asked for? If not, write below what you will ASK for, after reading this section.

Chapter Seven Fulfilling Your Passion, Purpose & Power In God

19. What is the theme scripture for chapter seven? Write it below and what it means to you.

20. Who is the featured heroine in chapter seven? Write her name below. What's the most important thing you've learned about her? Write it below, also.

21. The author proposed twelve energies that will continue to move us forward in fulfilling our destiny, successfully. Write below the top three that stood out to you the most. Briefly explain why they are meaningful to you.

1. The power of urgency.
2. The power of love.
3. The power of forgiveness.
4. The power of vision.
5. The power of clarity.
6. The power of excellence.
7. The power of diligence and hard work.
8. The power of compassion.

9. The power of enterprise.

10. The power of routine.

11. The power of perseverance.

12. The power of passing the torch.

21a. In chapter seven, the author outlined fifteen reasons why Jesus came to earth, all scripturally based. Which three were most meaning to you, write below. What do you consider your big why or your big purpose? Write below

23. Write below why you enjoyed the book WOW Women of Destiny. Do you feel Father God changed your life or heart in any specific way? Consider joining other WOW! Women who have wrote in with their testimony, write your words below and your testimony about the book at website http://wowontheweb.com

Go to your destiny,
Earma, 12 Book Christian Author, Founder of WOW! Women Global
http://www.wowontheweb.com

About Author

Carma Brown inspires women around the world to become women of destiny, purpose, and victory through speaking engagements, her books, Bible curriculum and studies. She is author of the trilogy of WOW! Women books: *Women of Worth, Women of Destiny* and *Women of Legacy*, along with the *Armorbearer Training Series*, *Prayer Fulfilled Life* books and *Writing A Book God's Way* book and course. She and her husband Varn live in Dallas Texas.

Other WOW! Women Books & Resources

WOW! Women of Worth (Book 1)

Have you feared you would never know why you are here? If so, you are not alone a Gallup poll has determined that one of people's greatest fears is to die having lived a meaningless life. With passion and grace, author Earma Brown declares there's no better place to look for answers than the Bible. She uncovers a biblical trail of seven strategies to becoming an extraordinary woman using ordinary tools. Her book *Women of Worth* will help you live a life full of meaning while understanding how to:

• Avoid the mistakes forever caused by low self-esteem.

• Overcome an enemy called insignificance.

• Defeat the dream assassins sent to kill your spirit and your dreams.

• Unlock the potential that many never tap into.

• Gain a sense of destiny that will change your life.

The Desire for a Bright Future! "Father God has put in each of us as a seed, the desire for a bright future," explains Earma. "I have designed the book to hopefully position the reader to receive God's plans to satisfy that longing," Start your journey today using the seven strategies in everything you do and experience the joy of becoming an extraordinary woman using ordinary tools.

WOW! Women of Legacy (Book 3)

How To Live Your Life As A Legacy

Are you designing your life as a torch? Your eye is on the next generation. Your heart is in tune with God. You desire to see the next generation do even better than this one. There's good news! You can live a life of legacy. God is a god of the generations. He is the same yesterday, today and forever. Through God's plan, this generation prepares and passes the torch to the next. Inside this book you will discover seven steps to prepare and live your life as a legacy:

- Discover A Woman's Pattern Of Power and learn to leave a legacy for generations to come.
- Uncover A Woman's Royal Call To Rule and tap into your inner queen.
- Engage In A Woman's War With Words And Break the generational curses threatening to destroy your family.
- Find A Woman's Will To Win And Overcome the Giants of Your Generation
- Form A Woman's Torch Of Legacy And prepare the torch of your life.
- Live A Woman's Life Well and Live the Legacy
- THRIVE, a discipleship and mentoring program for WOW! Women all over the world.

"Father God desires the same for each generation. He has put in each of us a blueprint, the thoughts, plans and desire for a bright future," explains Earma. "I have designed the WOW! Women of Legacy book to hopefully position the reader to receive God's plans, live it and pass it to the next generation," Start your journey today using the seven lessons in everything you do and experience the joy of designing your life, as a torch full of passion, purpose and legacy in God.

Practical and inspiring, WOW! Women of Legacy book three of the WOW Women Book Series is not only for women's groups. This book is a must read for Christian men and women alike seeking to empower their wives, sisters, mothers and daughters to fulfill their passion, purpose, power, and live their life as a legacy.

For more about the WOW Women Books and other WOW! Women resources, visit Earma at the WOW! Women Shop
http://wowontheweb.com/shop/

Notes

www.ingramcontent.com/pod-product-compliance
Lightning Source LLC
Chambersburg PA
CBHW030933090426
42737CB00007B/407